Central Park
The Early Years

Dianne L. Durante

Copyright © 2017 Dianne L. Durante
www.DianneDuranteWriter.com
www.ForgottenDelights.com
DuranteDianne@gmail.com
All rights reserved.

DESCRIPTION

It's difficult to imagine Manhattan without the glorious oasis that is Central Park. But the Park's existence was not inevitable, and its design was very much a product of its time. *Central Park: The Early Years* looks at why and how Central Park was created in the 1850s and its history during the formative decades of the 1860s and 1870s.

This book grew out of research for the seventy-three episodes of the Guides Who Know videoguide to Central Park. For a list of the episodes, see Chapter 9.

NOTES

The links (underlined in the text) are available in Chapter 11 (References) and online at http://diannedurantewriter.com/central-park-the-early-years-references

COVER

The 30 chromolithographic views of Central Park on the cover were issued by Louis Prang in 1864. I spotted them in a catalogue of William Reese Co. (https://www.williamreesecompany.com/): many thanks to Mr. Reese for sharing high-res photographs. The entire set of cards is printed n Chapter 12. Cover design: Allegra & Dianne Durante.

ABOUT THE AUTHOR

For more on the author, visit http://diannedurantewriter.com/about/ the Amazon Author Page for Dianne L. Durante, and my Patreon page at https://www.patreon.com/diannedurante.

I'm happy to hear comments, corrections, and suggestions, and I'll be delirious with delight if you write a review on Amazon.

First published in book form via CreateSpace, December 2017.
This issue published 6/18/2018.

Table of Contents

Chapter 1: Introduction 7
Chapter 2: New York Circa 1850 8
  2.1 Early History of Manhattan 8
  2.2 Why the City Grew 8
    2.2.1 Transportation hub 8
    2.2.2 Transfer point or destination for immigrants 11
    2.2.3 Manufacturing center 11
    2.2.4 Financial center 11
  2.3 High Points of New York Circa 1850 12
    2.3.1 Business and wealth 12
    2.3.2 Literacy and the search for knowledge 12
    2.3.3 Architecture 13
    2.3.4 Music 14
    2.3.5 Sculpture 15
    2.3.6 Painting 15
  2.4 Low Points of New York Circa 1850 16
    2.4.1 Prejudice and slavery 16
    2.4.2 Corruption in city government 16
    2.4.3 Overcrowding 18
    2.4.4 Health hazards 18
Chapter 3: Sidling Toward a Park 23
  3.1 Why Build a Park? 23
    3.1.1 Fresh air and exercise 23
    3.1.2 Pastoral views 23
    3.1.3 Culture 24
  3.2 Where? 24
  3.3 The Site before the Park 26
    3.3.1 Homes and businesses 26
    3.3.2 Institutions 26
    3.3.3 Topography 28

Chapter 4: Players and Plans..30
  4.1 Egbert Ludovicus Viele 30
  4.2 Frederick Law Olmsted 32
  4.3 Calvert Vaux 35
  4.4 The Design Competition..36
  4.5 The Greensward Plan...36
Chapter 5: Construction of Central Park..42
  5.1 Execution of the Greensward Plan 42
  5.2 Early Revisions to the Greensward Plan 44
    5.2.1 The Extension, 106th-110th Streets 44
    5.2.2 The Bow Bridge 46
    5.2.3 The circulation system 47
  5.3 Finances: Andrew Haswell Green 48
Chapter 6: Architectural Elements in Central Park..........................51
  6.1 Bethesda Terrace...51
  6.2 The Belvedere...54
  6.3 The Dairy 56
  6.4 The Zoo...58
  6.5 The Sheepfold...61
  6.6 The American Museum of Natural History 63
  6.7 The Metropolitan Museum of Art...63
  6.8 Wall and Gates 66
Chapter 7: Sculptures in Central Park..69
  7.1 Earliest Sculptures 69
    7.1.1 Bethesda Fountain, dedicated 1873 (Emma
       Stebbins)..69
    7.1.2 Schiller, 1869 (C.L. Richter)...71
    7.1.3 Eagles and Prey, 1863 (Christophe Fratin) 71
    7.1.4 Tigress with Cubs, 1866 (Auguste Cain) 72
    7.1.5 Indian Hunter, 1866 (John Quincy Adams Ward).........73
    7.1.6 Seventh Regiment Memorial, 1869 (John Quincy
       Adams Ward)..73
    7.1.7 Humboldt, 1869 (Gustaf Blaeser) 74
    7.1.8 Morse, 1871 (Byron M. Pickett) 74
    7.1.9 Scott, 1871 (Sir John Steell) 75

    7.1.10 Shakespeare, 1872 (John Quincy Adams Ward) 75
    7.1.11 The Falconer, 1875 (George Blackall Simonds) 76
  7.2 Board of Commissioners' Rules on Sculpture, 1873 76
  7.3 The Halleck Fiasco, 1877 77
Chapter 8: The Tweed Years, 1870-1871, and Their Effects 80
  8.1 Boss Tweed and His Cronies 80
  8.2 Effects of Tweed's Reign 82
Chapter 9: Episodes in the Guides Who Know Central Park App ... 85
Chapter 10: Further Readings 87
Chapter 11: References 89
Chapter 12: 1865 Chromolithographs of Central Park
  by Louis Prang 92

CHAPTER 1
Introduction

I'm fascinated by the choices and chances that bring about what we think of as "inevitable". Take Central Park. Although it's difficult to imagine Manhattan without a glorious oasis in its center, the Park's existence, its location, and its design were much debated. *Central Park: The Early Years* looks at why and how Central Park was created in the 1850s, and its development during the formative decades of the 1860s and 1870s. Included are many quotes from those who worked on the park and more than a hundred early photographs and images of the Park.

Among the topics:
- The context: New York circa 1850
- The original aim of the Park
- The most important figures in the Park's early history
- The construction of the Park
- Early buildings and sculptures in the Park
- The Tweed years and their effects

Fig. 1: Image of Bethesda Terrace from the Annual Report of the Board of Commissioners of the Central Park for 1859. *The illustration is signed by Jacob Wrey Mould as artist.*

CHAPTER 2
New York Circa 1850

2.1 THE EARLY HISTORY OF MANHATTAN

By the early 1850s, when a major park for Manhattan was first discussed, the island had been settled by Europeans for more than two centuries. It offered a unique combination on the east coast of America: a well-protected, deep-water harbor that was never closed off by ice, and a river that was navigable inland for some two hundred miles. The Dutch trading post of New Amsterdam, founded in 1624, began as a fort and a few houses near the harbor, and grew northward (Fig. 2).

As a successful trading center, Manhattan was a target. In 1664, four British warships sailed into the harbor and forced Peter Stuyvesant to surrender the town. New Amsterdam became New York.

The town continued to prosper under British control, although it remained small. When the Declaration of Independence was read to a cheering crowd at the Common (now City Hall Park) in 1776, most of the town's buildings still huddled south of Fulton Street (Figs. 3, 4).

During the Revolutionary War, the British occupied New York for seven years. When they evacuated in 1783, the town was crippled. A fire had destroyed a third of its buildings. (That's the shaded area in Fig. 4.) Soldiers had used public buildings as barracks and stables. Every tree and bush on the island had been burned for fuel. The town's wharves—its lifeline, its link to global commerce—were collapsing into the rivers.

2.2 WHY THE CITY GREW

How did New York rise from literal ashes to become America's most populous city?

2.2.1 Transportation hub

The harbor and river made Manhattan a hub for transatlantic trade and trade with upstate New York. The mind and muscle of men made the island the hub of an even larger network. In 1825, after eight years of construction, the Erie Canal opened for business. Starting on the

CENTRAL PARK: THE EARLY YEARS

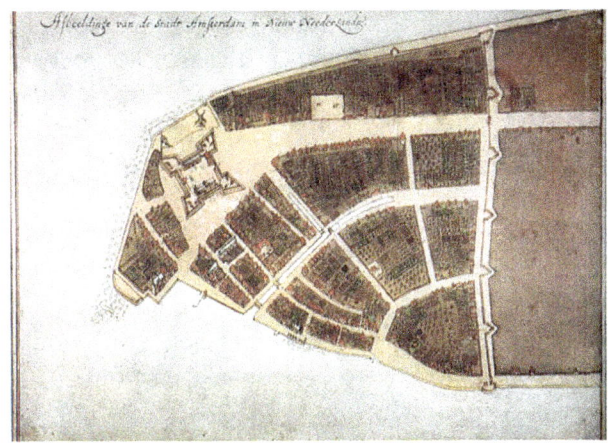

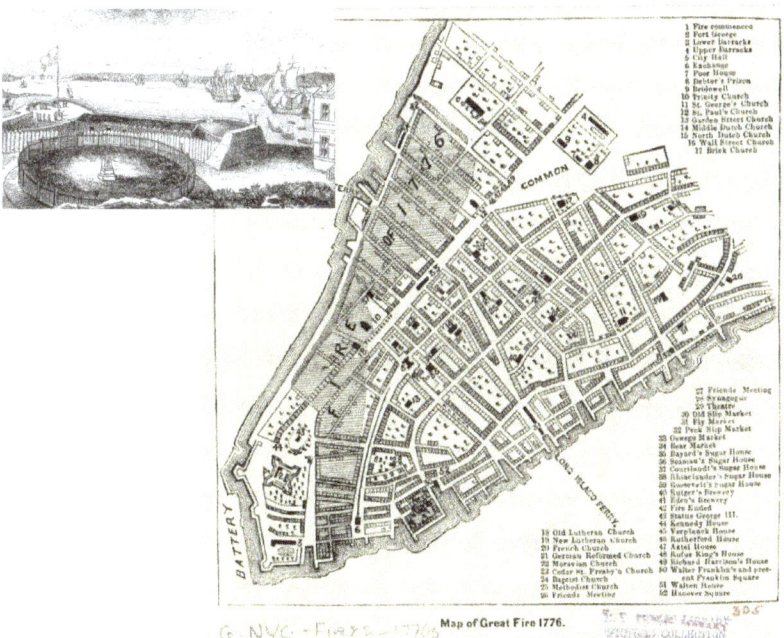

Fig. 2: The Castello Plan of Manhattan, 1660. The wall at the north edge of the settlement (to the right) is modern Wall Street. Image: Wikipedia

Fig. 3: Fort George, once at the southern tip of Manhattan, now beneath the Alexander Hamilton U.S. Customs House. Image: Wikipedia

Fig. 4: Lower Manhattan, 1776. The Common, near the top right, eventually became City Hall Park. The Battery (with the town's cannons) and the fort face the harbor, toward the lower left. The shading on the left marks the area destroyed by the Great Fire of 1776. Image: New York Public Library Digital Collections

Hudson River just north of Albany, the Canal ran through the only water-level pass in the northern end of the Appalachian Mountains, then continued west to Buffalo, on Lake Erie. From there, ships could navigate through the Great Lakes to the Midwest (Fig. 5).

In the Midwest, farmland was far more plentiful and fertile than on the long-settled Atlantic coast. But how could farmers transport surplus produce to the population centers of the East? Until 1825, they had only two choices. They could load it on a horse-drawn cart and send it overland through the Appalachians. Or they could load it on a boat and send it down the Mississippi River, around the tip of Florida, and up the East Coast. Both options were expensive, and so time-consuming that spoilage was a problem.

The Erie Canal provided a much cheaper and faster option. Produce shipped to New York could be consumed here, or easily shipped elsewhere. On the return trip, canal boats carried manufactured goods and other necessities to farmers in the Midwest.

In 1851, the first railroad from New York to Lake Erie opened for business, on tracks laid next to the Erie Canal. Suddenly the cost of shipping freight from Buffalo to New York dropped from $100 to $10 per ton. Travel time dropped from twenty-six to six days.

Fig. 5: The United States in 1853, with the Erie Canal, the Hudson River, New York, and the Mississippi River highlighted. Original image: David Rumsey Map Collection

By the early 1850s, as a result of the Erie Canal and the railroads, a third of America's exports left from New York's harbor. Half the goods imported to the United States entered the country here, to be consumed or shipped onward.

2.2.2 Transfer point or destination for immigrants

Stories of the rich lands of the Midwest attracted hundreds of thousands of European immigrants, who sailed into New York Harbor as the first stop on their way west. Many chose to remain here and work in manufacturing or construction. By 1860, 47% of the population of Manhattan was foreign-born. It's no coincidence that the first sculpture erected in Central Park was to a German playwright (Chapter 7.1.2.)

2.2.3 Manufacturing center

With freight rates plummeting due to the Erie Canal and the railroads, it became cost-effective to ship raw materials to New York and manufacture goods here. The city's rapidly growing population provided an ample labor force. For well over a century, factories and warehouses jammed the blocks next to the wharves in Manhattan and Brooklyn, so that finished goods could be loaded directly onto ships.

Since the early twenty-first century, decrepit factories and warehouses along the East River have been replaced by residential towers with fantastic views. The reason? Container ships. Containers are such efficient transportation that goods can be produced where labor and real estate are cheaper than in New York City. But in the 1850s, waterfront property was still in high demand for shipping and manufacturing facilities—and that was an important factor in the choice of site for Central Park.

2.2.4 Financial center

In the early nineteenth century, a Philadelphian who wanted shares in a company traded in New York would have arranged the purchase through a stock exchange in Philadelphia. By 1850, a network of telegraph lines allowed near-instantaneous communication between New York and other major cities on the East Coast. The telegraph made local exchanges obsolete and transformed Wall Street, home of the New York Stock Exchange, into America's financial capital.

So: by the early 1850s, New York was a transportation hub, a transfer point or destination for immigrants, a manufacturing center, and a financial center. All that brought the city great benefits ... and serious problems.

2.3 HIGH POINTS OF NEW YORK CIRCA 1850

New York had many positive aspects in the mid-nineteenth century, including developments in business, science, technology, and the arts.

2.3.1 Business and wealth

By 1844, John Jacob Astor, Cornelius Vanderbilt, Peter Cooper, A.T. Stewart, and twenty more New Yorkers were millionaires. These men made their fortunes by providing goods and services that New Yorkers wanted. Their companies helped provide the jobs that made the city a magnet for immigrants.

2.3.2 Literacy and the search for knowledge

In the mid-nineteenth century, the average child was out of school by age fourteen. Yet New Yorkers read voraciously. When the first issues of *Harper's Weekly* and the *New York Times* rolled off the presses in 1851, they joined thirty or forty other newspapers, among them Horace Greeley's *New-York Tribune* and James Gordon Bennett's *New-York Herald*. New York was also the headquarters of dozens of book publishers, including Scribner's, Putnam's, and Appleton's. Washington Irving, William Cullen Bryant, Herman Melville, and Walt Whitman were all living and writing in New York in the decade of the 1850s.

The New York area was also becoming a center of learning and research. Charles Pfizer established what is now Pfizer Corporation in Williamsburgh in 1849. Dr. James Marion Sims, the "Father of Gynecology," settled here in 1853; two years later, he founded one of the first women's hospitals in the United States (Fig. 6). Isaac Merritt Singer patented his sewing machine in New York in 1851, and established I.M. Singer & Company to mass-produce it. In 1849, John Jacob Astor bequeathed money for the Astor Library—the first privately endowed, independent, free research library in the United States, and the seed of the New York Public Library.

Fig. 6: Monument honoring Dr. J. Marion Sims, Fifth Avenue at 103rd St. Photo copyright © 2017 Dianne L. Durante. See also my Dr. James Marion Sims, with Notes on New York's Sculpture of Sims.

2.3.3 Architecture

In 1849, James Bogardus erected the first cast-iron building (Fig. 7). In 1854, the Otis Safety Elevator was demonstrated to gaping crowds at the New York World's Fair (Fig. 8). The combination of cast-iron (later steel) construction and elevators made taller buildings feasible. By 1915, the lower end of Manhattan was filled with skyscrapers (Fig. 9).

Fig. 7: Kitchen, Montross & Wilcox Store at 85 Leonard Street, a cast-iron building by James Bogardus, 1861. Image: Beyond My Ken / Wikipedia

Fig. 8: Demonstration of the Otis Safety Elevator in 1854. Image: Wikipedia

Fig. 9: Bird's-eye view of lower Manhattan in 1915. Image: Library of Congress

2.3.4 Music

For musicians as well as writers, New York was a magnet. The New York Philharmonic opened its doors in 1842, the Astor Place Opera House in 1847, Steinway & Sons piano factory in 1853, and the New York Academy of Music in 1854.

Music was not just for the wealthy elite. In 1850, circus entrepreneur P.T. Barnum persuaded Jenny Lind—the "Swedish nightingale"—to tour the United States. Lind sang music that many today consider demanding: opera and art songs. A crowd of thirty or forty thousand greeted Lind at the dock in New York. Her face and figure were plastered on everything from paper dolls to tobacco packets (Figs. 10, 11).

Fig. 10: Jenny Lind paper doll. Image: New-York Historical Society

Fig. 11: Jenny Lind tobacco. Image: Library of Congress

Fig. 12: Henry Kirke Brown, George Washington, *dedicated 1856. Photo copyright © 2014 Dianne L. Durante*

CENTRAL PARK: THE EARLY YEARS   15

2.3.5 Sculpture

In 1856, the year that land for Central Park began to be cleared, the sculpture of George Washington at Union Square was dedicated (Fig. 12). It was the first monumental sculpture to stand in Manhattan since the gilded sculpture of King George III was hauled off its pedestal in July 1776. *Washington* was paid for not by the government, but by a group of merchants. It was designed by an American, Henry Kirke Brown, and the bronze was cast in America. This sort of realistic detail became a trademark of American sculpture.

2.3.6 Painting

The most prominent group of American painters from 1825 to 1875 was the Hudson River School. Artists such as Thomas Cole, Asher B. Durand, Frederic Church, and Jasper Cropsey showed nature as mysterious but not malevolent. Their attitude was: We can look at nature and enjoy it, or we can explore, tame, and settle it (Figs. 13, 14). This view of nature was very influential on the designers of Central Park.

Fig. 13: Asher B. Durand, Kindred Spirits, *1849. Collection Crystal Bridges Museum of American Art, Bentonville, AR.*

Fig. 14: Thomas Cole, View from Mount Holyoke, Northampton, Massachusetts, after a Thunderstorm - The Oxbow, *1836. Metropolitan Museum of Art, Gift of Mrs. Russell Sage, 1908. Photo: MetMuseum.org*

2.4 LOW POINTS OF NEW YORK CIRCA 1850

Business, science, technology, and the arts were thriving in New York around 1850—but the city was hardly an earthly paradise.

2.4.1 Prejudice and slavery

Many New Yorkers of the mid-nineteenth century had strong prejudices against blacks and recent immigrants. The 1850s were the peak of membership in the American Party, often referred to as the "Know Nothing" party. The Know Nothings opposed immigrants and Catholics, and generally anyone who was non-white and non-northern-European. Their candidate, Millard Fillmore, was elected president of the United States in 1856.

Across America, the slavery issue continued to fester, as it had since the Constitution was written in 1787. According to the Compromise of 1850, slavery would not be allowed in the new state of California. Other western territories were allowed to choose whether to permit slavery. The Compromise included the Fugitive Slave Act, which mandated that slaves who had escaped to the North were to be returned to their owners. Frederick Douglas had escaped to New York in 1838 (Fig. 15). Under the Fugitive Slave Act, he could have been captured and returned to his "master" in Maryland (Fig. 17).

Among Northerners, slavery remained a divisive issue. Daniel Webster had been praised as a hero for his 1830 speech opposing states' rights to nullify federal laws. But Webster, who had been a vocal abolitionist, spoke in favor of the Compromise of 1850, hoping it would save the United States from civil war: "There can be no such thing as peaceable secession." His former friends immediately became his bitter enemies. John Greenleaf Whittier wrote,

> All else is gone; from those great eyes
> The soul has fled:
> When faith is lost, when honor dies,
> The man is dead.

Central Park's sculpture of Webster (Fig. 16) wasn't erected until a full decade after the Civil War, when the United States was celebrating the centennial of its independence.

2.4.2 Corruption in city government

Prejudice wasn't the only problem in New York during the mid-nineteenth century. In the 1840s, the forty members of the city's governing

Fig. 15: Gabriel Koren, Frederick Douglas, *2011. Central Park West at 110th Street. Photo copyright © 2016 Dianne L. Durante*

Fig. 16: Thomas Ball, Daniel Webster, *1876. Central Park, west side near the 72nd Street entrance. The inscription includes the most famous words from his 1830 speech: "Liberty and Union, now and forever, one and inseparable!" Photo copyright © 2017 Dianne L. Durante*

Fig. 17: Poster created in Boston in 1851, following the Fugitive Slave Act. Source: Wikipedia

council were nicknamed the "Forty Thieves". They ran the government by the spoils system, handing out jobs to friends, family, and flunkies, qualified or not. They skimmed funds. They cheated at elections. In 1851, William Magear Tweed ("Boss Tweed") was elected to the Board of Aldermen of New York for the first time. He consolidated his power during the 1850s and 1860s, and in the 1870s had a major impact on Central Park (Chapter 8).

2.4.3 Overcrowding

Another urgent problem in Manhattan was the living conditions of its burgeoning population, which doubled in size every twenty years or so. In 1850, most of Manhattan's population of half a million lived and worked south of 42nd Street (Figs. 18, 19).

They had little choice. There were no cars, no subways, no local railroads. The only mass transit was slow-moving, horse-drawn cars. For low-paid laborers who worked ten-hour days, it wasn't feasible to live anywhere except southern Manhattan.

But they were jammed into it. A standard building lot in Manhattan is 25 x 100 feet. A five- or six-story building on such a lot typically had four families per floor. That meant parents and children shared a space about 25 x 25 feet. You could fit three such spaces onto one of today's regulation tennis courts, or ninety-two of them on a football field.

If you wonder why anyone tolerated such conditions, visit the Irish Hunger Memorial in downtown Manhattan. The Memorial includes a typical Irish stone cottage from the mid-nineteenth century: a single room without windowpanes or plumbing, heated by a fireplace. Living in such a "quaint" cottage involved working outdoors from dawn to dusk, no matter what the weather—for bare subsistence, and often not even that. By comparison, a cramped row house in Manhattan with glass windows, running water, and heat, paid for with a mere ten-hour day in a factory, was bliss.

2.4.4 Health hazards

Although a row house was better than a stone hut, by today's standards, health conditions in New York City circa 1850 were abysmal. But efforts were being made to improve them. In 1842, the Croton Aqueduct began carrying fresh water to the city from Westchester, forty-one miles north of Manhattan. The aqueduct was an engineering

CENTRAL PARK: THE EARLY YEARS 19

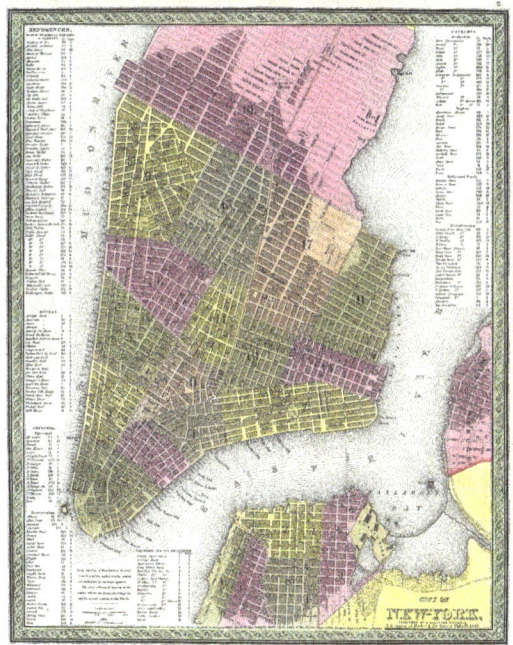

Fig. 18: View north from St. Paul's Church in lower Manhattan, 1848. Image: Metropolitan Museum of Art, The Edward W. C. Arnold Collection of New York Prints, Maps and Pictures, Bequest of Edward W. C. Arnold, 1954

Fig. 19: Map of the built-up parts of Manhattan, ca. 1848. Image: Wikipedia

marvel, built in seven years without electricity or gas-powered engines (Figs. 20, 21).

Water from the Croton Reservoir flowed downhill, crossing the High Bridge in upper Manhattan, thence to the Receiving Reservoir in the middle of Manhattan, and from there to the neo-Egyptian Distributing Reservoir in Bryant Park (Figs. 23, 22, 24, 25). Then it flowed to the built-up areas in lower Manhattan. The opening of the Croton Aqueduct was celebrated with a gigantic geyser in the fountain at City Hall Park (Fig. 26).

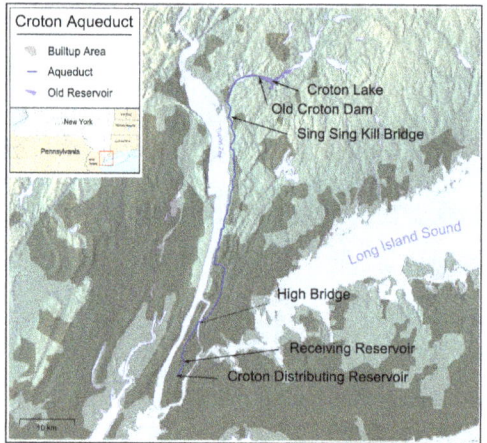

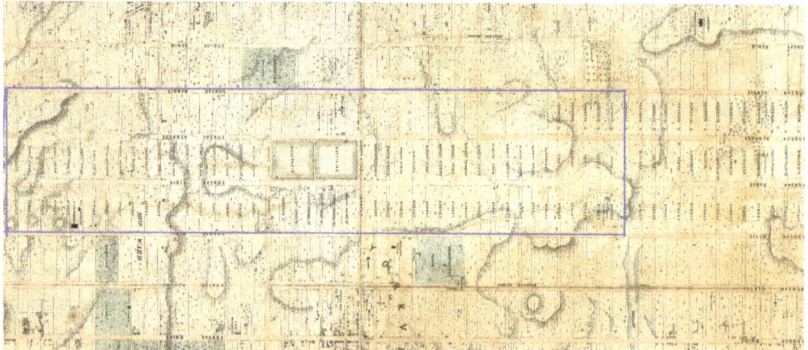

Fig. 20: The Croton Aqueduct route. Image: Wikipedia

Fig. 21: Some of the machinery for controlling the flow of water in the Croton Aqueduct. Image: Harper's Weekly, 1881

Fig. 22: The Receiving Reservoir for the Croton Aqueduct, between 79th and 86th Streets and 6th and 7th Avenues. The area that became Central Park is outlined in blue. Image: 1851 Dripps Map of Manhattan, courtesy David Rumsey Map Collection.

CENTRAL PARK: THE EARLY YEARS

Fig. 23: The High Bridge over the East River, at about West 173rd Street, as originally designed (1840s). Image: Charles Hemstreet, When Old New York was Young, *1902*

Fig. 24: Receiving Reservoir, where Central Park's Great Lawn is now. The walls were wide enough to form a promenade. Part of the north wall is still in place behind the police precinct on the 86th Street Transverse. Image: New York Public Library Digital Collections

Fig. 25: Neo-Egyptian style Distributing Reservoir, between 40th and 42nd Streets (present Bryant Park), in 1866. Image: Benson John Lossing, The Hudson from the Wilderness to the Sea, *1866*

Fig. 26: Water from the Croton Aqueduct gushing out of the fountain at City Hall Park, 1842. Image: New York Public Library Digital Collections

The Croton Aqueduct delivered huge quantities of clean drinking water, and the availability of such water did much to improve public health. But the aqueduct did not provide enough water to carry away sewage—and Manhattan was full of sewage. The contents of backyard outhouses seeped into the ground. The streets were full of horse excrement. If you've ever been on Central Park South during a hot summer day, you know that ten horses are enough to create a stink. In Manhattan in 1850, there were more than twenty thousand working horses. Most of them lived south of 42nd Street, near the humans who owned them,.

Not only that: when your horse, cow, or dog died, it stayed with you until someone came to haul it off. In August 1853—one month!—the city's contract scavenger cleared away:

- 577 horses
- 690 cows
- 883 dogs
- 111 cats
- 14 hogs
- 6 sheep
- 1,300 tons of butcher's offal
- 62 tons of bones from slaughterhouses

Given the amount of sewage and garbage oozing into the water supply, it's no surprise that waterborne diseases were widespread in Manhattan. In the 1849 cholera epidemic, five thousand people died—one percent of the city's population. It was clear by 1850 that the Croton Aqueduct needed a second, much larger reservoir to handle the city's demands for water. That, too, had an effect on Central Park.

CHAPTER 3
Sidling Toward a Park

3.1 WHY BUILD A PARK?

By the late 1840s, many of Manhattan's tycoons, industrialists, culture mavens, scientists, artists, writers, and painters agreed that Manhattan needed a park. As the Board of Commissioners noted in 1860, when construction had just begun, the Park was

> intended to furnish healthful recreation for the poor and the rich, the young and the old, the vicious and the virtuous, so far as each can partake therein without infringing upon the rights of others, and no further. (*Fourth Annual Report of the Board of Commissioners of the Central Park, January 1861,* p. 113.)

But there were several very different conceptions of what "healthful recreation" involved. Those ideas are the threads that weave, braid, and tangle through Central Park's history, decade after decade.

3.1.1 Fresh air and exercise

In the 1850s, people didn't know that germs were the cause of disease; but it was obvious that disease spread more quickly in close quarters. It was also obvious that people who moved about, played, and exercised tended to be healthier. So one of the factions wanted the park to be a place where Manhattan residents could indulge in "agreeable exercise … as a relief from the confinement of houses and streets. This will be obtained by the mass of the community, by riding, driving, or walking …" (*Fourth Annual Report of the Board of Commissioners of the Central Park, January 1861,* p. 117).

3.1.2 Pastoral views

Another faction argued that it was intrinsically good for people to see broad, sweeping views that weren't restricted by the city's unrelentingly rectangular grid plan. Brooklyn offered the beautifully landscaped acres of the Green-Wood Cemetery, opened in 1838—a wonderful place for a stroll in the "country". But reaching the Green-Wood from Manhattan meant getting to the shore, taking a ferry, and then travelling another five miles. Manhattanites should have easier access to that sort of pastoral landscape, said this faction.

3.1.3 Culture

As the Industrial Revolution progressed in the United States, Manhattan became home to an increasing number of wealthy and educated people, from railroad tycoons to book publishers to manufacturers. These people were eager to make New York a world-class city. London and Paris have great parks: New York should, too! And, they argued, a well-designed and well-maintained park will help civilize the poor, like taking a child to a nice restaurant. The underprivileged will learn by example how to behave.

These were the three factions who favored a major Manhattan park: those who thought it should provide a place for fresh air and exercise, those who wanted a pastoral setting, and those who wanted it to display New York's increasingly high level of culture. By the early 1850s, the combination of all these groups meant that a significant number of influential New Yorkers considered a park desirable. Down the road, as we'll see, they would have to settle the fact that their desires and expectations were not necessarily compatible.

3.2 WHERE?

Where should the park be located? The grid of Manhattan's streets, laid out in 1811, included spaces for a few parks, left in white on the "Commissioners' Plan" (Fig. 27). By 1850, however, land below 42nd Street was far too valuable to leave undeveloped.

The possible locations for a large park were quickly narrowed down to two (Fig. 28). Although the benefits of the park for the lower classes were mentioned, neither of the sites was easily accessible to the struggling poor on the crowded Lower East Side.

The first potential site was Jones Wood, which ran from 66th Street to 70th Street and from Third Avenue to the East River.

The other possible location was a parcel five times as large as Jones Wood, laid out symmetrically around the original Croton Reservoir. It ran from 59th to 106th Streets and from Fifth to Eighth Avenues, incorporating the site that had already been chosen for a new, much larger reservoir, just north of the original one. This block of land was less desirable for development: hilly, rocky, and far from the busy shores of the Hudson and East Rivers.

In 1853, the New York State legislature (which supervised New York City's affairs) gave New York City the power to purchase both

CENTRAL PARK: THE EARLY YEARS

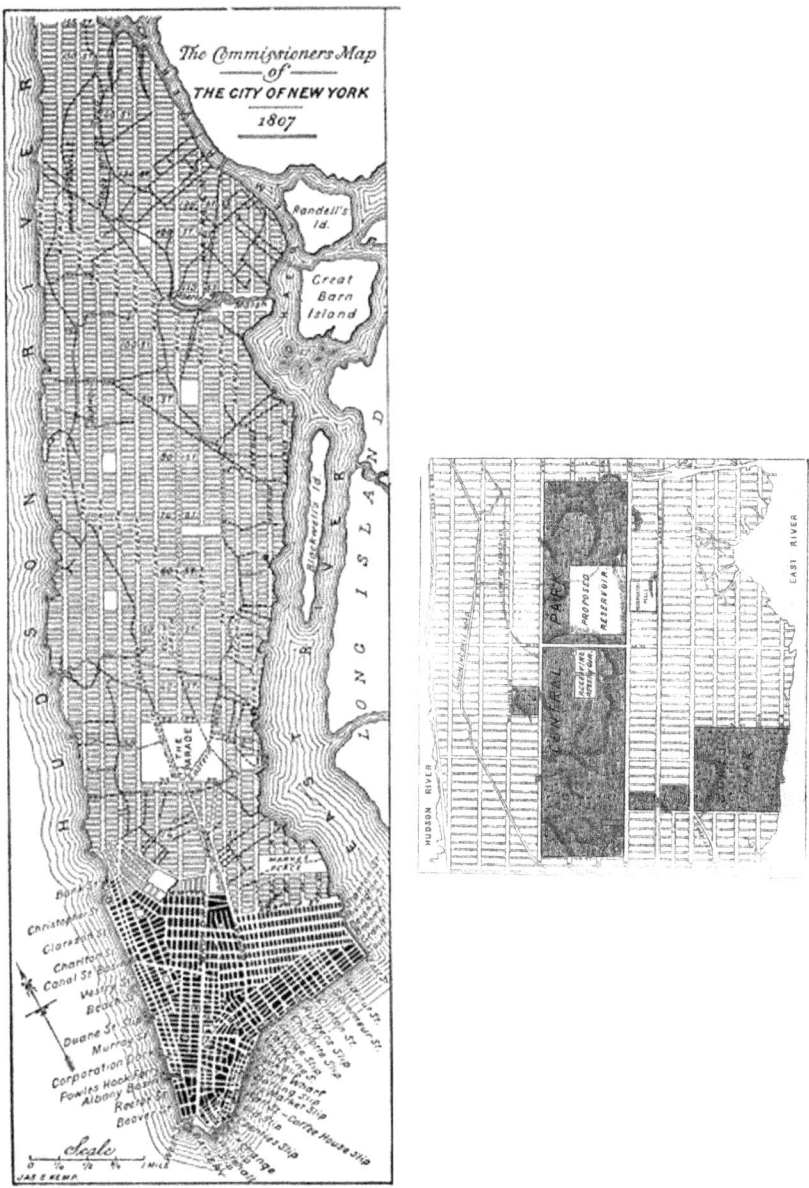

Fig. 27: Commissioners' Plan of Manhattan, 1811. The regular grid begins in the area that was sparsely settled at the time, north of Greenwich Village. Image: Wikipedia

Fig. 28: Map of 1853, from 57th to 109th Streets, showing two proposed sites for Manhattan's park. Image: New-York Historical Society

Jones Wood and the larger central parcel. A year later, the legislature revoked the right to purchase Jones Wood. The city's new park would be "the Central Park".

The city sent out surveyors and appraisers to examine some 34,000 lots on the future park's site. Their owners received an average of $700 per lot. The cost to purchase the land came to about $5 million. Eminent domain was invoked for anyone who refused to sell.

3.3 THE SITE BEFORE THE PARK

3.3.1 Homes and businesses

The block of land slated for Central Park included only one settlement: Seneca Village, on the west side of the park at about West 85th Street. Its residents included about three hundred free African-Americans and a handful of immigrants. All of them were forced to move.

At the south end of the park were odoriferous businesses that no one wanted downtown, such as pig sties, slaughterhouses, distillery dairies (see Chapter 6.3), and bone-boiling works. "A suburb more filthy, squalid, and disgusting can hardly be imagined," said the Board of Commissioners in their _Fourth Annual Report, January 1861_ (p. 111).

3.3.2 Institutions

Near the north end of the park site stood the Academy of Mount Saint Vincent, established in 1847 by the Sisters of Charity for the education of women. The Sisters relocated to Riverdale in 1859, and their former home became a tavern, restaurant, and art gallery in Central Park. It was destroyed by fire in 1881 (Figs. 29, 30, 31). All that remains are a few stones from the foundation, on the hill behind the Conservatory Garden.

The only building on the original park site that's still standing is the Arsenal (Fig. 32). It had been constructed for the New York State Militia in 1851. Although its battlements give it the appearance of a castle, it wasn't defensible: a cannonball or an explosive shell would have blown right through the walls. The Arsenal was designed to store gunpowder and cannonballs near the center of the island. From there, they could quickly be sent off to any part of Manhattan that was under attack.

Once the surrounding area was chosen for the city's park, it was wisely decided not to store gunpowder in the Arsenal. The city bought the building from New York State. We'll see what they did with it later (Chapter 6.4).

CENTRAL PARK: THE EARLY YEARS 27

Fig. 29: Mount Saint Vincent in 1869: "The Museum and Restaurant from Harlem Meer". Image: Clarence Cook, A Description of the New York Central Park, *1869*

Fig. 30: Mount Saint Vincent after the fire, 1881. Image: CopyrightExpired. com

Fig. 31: Statuary Hall: Sculptures in the old chapel of Mount Saint Vincent, 1860s or 1870s. Image: New York Public Library Digital Collections

Fig. 32: The Arsenal in 1866. Image: CopyrightExpired.com

3.3.3 Topography

The rest of the Central Park site was not promising, as contemporary views show (Figs. 34, 35).

At the south end of the Park, two streams ran east-west. Around them was a swampy area; between them, a rocky ridge. Manhattan's bedrock was so close to the surface, noted the Board of Commissioners, that "probably not a square rood [roughly 100 x 100 feet] could be found throughout which a crowbar could be thrust its length into the ground without encountering rock." (*Fourth Annual Report, January 1861*, p. 112.) A visitor to the southern end of the park site in August 1857 recalled his first impression:

> It was a sultry afternoon in the height of dog-days, and my conductor exhibited his practical ability by leading me through the midst of a number of vile sloughs, in the black and unctuous slime of which I sometimes sank nearly half-leg deep. ...
>
> [My guide] said but one word to me during the afternoon beyond what his commission strictly required. As I stopped for an instant to kick the mire off my legs against a stump, as we came out of the last bog, he turned and remarked: "Suppose you are used to this sort of business?" ...
>
> I avoided a direct reply by saying that I had not been aware that the park was such a very nasty place. In fact, the low grounds were steeped in the overflow and mush of pig-sties, slaughter houses and bone-boiling works, and the stench was sickening. (The source of this quote is given in Chapter 4.2.)

Between 79th and 86th Streets was the original Receiving Reservoir. North of that was the site for the new, much larger reservoir, which would occupy almost the entire width of the Park. Above 96th Street, at the north end of the Park, were several more streams, another swamp, and several huge, rocky outcrops (Fig. 33).

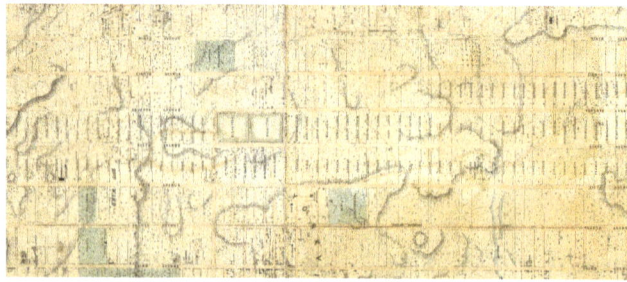

Fig. 33: 1851 Dripps map, showing topographical features; Central Park is outlined in blue. North is to the right. Image: David Rumsey Map Collection

CENTRAL PARK: THE EARLY YEARS 29

Fig. 34: Sketch of part of the land incorporated into Central Park, 1847. Image: New York Public Library Digital Collections

Fig. 35: Jervis McEntee, view from what became Bethesda Terrace, 1858. Image: National Building Museum.net

CHAPTER 4
Players and Plans

So: New York owns this swampy, smelly, rocky plot of ground. What should be done with it?

4.1 EGBERT LUDOVICUS VIELE

Enter Egbert Ludovicus Viele (Fig. 36), an army engineer who became one of the "Founding Fathers" of Central Park. In the early 1850s, when New Yorkers began to discuss creating a large park for Manhattan, Viele did a detailed topographical survey of the area that became Central Park (Fig. 37). He assumed that natural features should be taken into consideration when designing the park.

By 1856, Viele had been appointed engineer-in-chief of Central Park by the Board of Commissioners of Central Park. The Board, which remained the Park's governing body until the early twentieth century, consisted of two to eleven men who were appointed by the New York State legislature. One of the best sources for the early history of the Park is the Board's minutes and annual reports, which fill thousands of pages.

The very first annual report of the Board of Commissioners, issued in 1857, included Viele's "Plan for the improvement of The Central Park, Adopted by the Commissioners, June 3rd 1856" (Fig. 38).

To give you a sense of Viele's approach, here's his description of what the southeast corner of the Park would look like.

Fig. 36: Egbert Ludovicus Viele (1825-1902) in the 1860s. Image: National Archives and Record Administration

CENTRAL PARK: THE EARLY YEARS

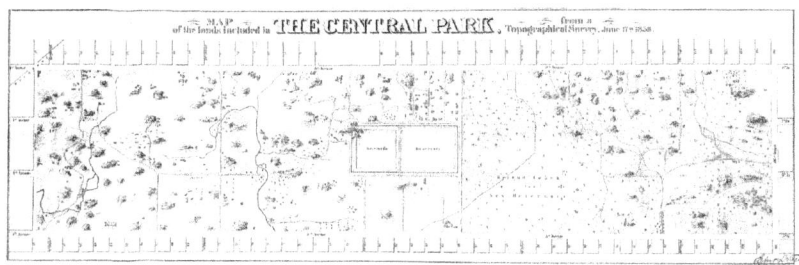

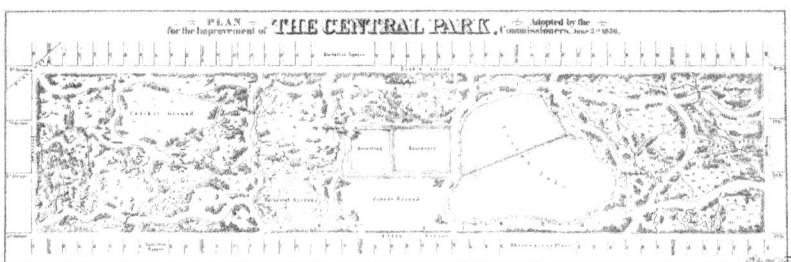

Fig. 37: Viele's topographical survey of Central Park, mid-1850s. North is to the right. Image: First Annual Report on the Improvement of the Central Park, New York, *1857*

Fig. 38: Viele's plan for Central Park, 1856. Image: First Annual Report on the Improvement of the Central Park, New York, *1857*

> The Circuit, or principal drive, is the main feature,—this enters the Park at the corner of Fifth-avenue and Fifty-ninth-street, with a roadway 70 feet in width, and a foot-path on either side of 15 feet, descending immediately by an easy grade, into a deep valley. On the left is a lake which terminates the stream running through this valley. On the right, a ledge of rocks. For a distance of about 150 feet, with a curve of 200 feet radius, it follows the base of a rock rising abruptly on the right, thence along the edge of a stream, coming in view of another sheet of water, with a cascade in the distance. (Viele, quoted in the *New York Times* 2/20/1857)

Aside from his attention to topography, the most notable feature of Viele's plan was his solution to the problem caused by the size and shape of the Park. The Park was only three blocks wide east to west, but forty-seven blocks long north to south. If no traffic were allowed through it, the Park would be a barricade between the east and west sides of Manhattan. But commercial traffic galloping through the Park would make it much less park-like, and dangerous to visitors who were enjoying a leisurely excursion. Viele's solution: five transverse roads through the park that were dedicated to commercial traffic.

In the summer of 1856, after Viele's plan for the Park was approved by the Commissioners and the owners of the lots were paid, a crew began clearing the land. By October 1857, about 1,600 residents had been evicted. The shanties that had been their homes were razed.

4.2 FREDERICK LAW OLMSTED

After Viele, the next important figure on the scene in Central Park was Frederick Law Olmsted (1822-1903, Fig. 39).

In 1857, thirty-five-year-old Olmsted had more knowledge of public parks than anyone else in the United States. Most Americans who traveled to Europe made the grand tour of palaces and museums in Paris, London, Berlin, and Rome. Olmsted headed instead for Liverpool's Birkenhead Park.

Until the mid-nineteenth century, parks in Europe were lands that belonged to royalty or nobles, who sometimes allowed the public to visit. Birkenhead was the first park built for the public, with public funds. It didn't evolve: it was designed (Figs. 40, 41, 42).

Olmsted studied Birkenhead Park's entrances, roads, and paths. He studied its drainage, its manmade ponds, its turf, bridges, and cricket grounds. Then he published his observations in *Walks and Talks of an American Farmer*, 1852 (Figs. 43, 44). *Walks and Talks* instantly made him the foremost American authority on public parks—indeed, the only American authority.

In the 1850s, Olmsted was living on a farm in Staten Island that he had transformed into a showcase. A friend on the Park's Board of Commissioners thought Olmsted, with his knowledge of public parks, ought to be involved in the creation of Central Park. Since all the seats on the Board had been filled, his

Fig. 39: Olmsted in 1850, age 28.
Image: Wikipedia

CENTRAL PARK: THE EARLY YEARS 33

Fig. 40: Map of Birkenhead Park, 1879. Image: Wikipedia
Fig. 41: View of Birkenhead Park. Image: Wikipedia
Fig. 42: Lake in Birkenhead Park. Image: Wikipedia

friend suggested that Olmsted apply for the position of park superintendent, who managed the workmen and the park police.

Olmsted was hired as park superintendent in August 1857 (Fig. 45). His boss was Egbert Ludovicus Viele—who told Olmsted that he would have preferred a "practical man" as superintendent. That description of the Park site as filled with "black unctuous slime" and a "very nasty place" (Chapter 3.3) was Olmsted's description of his first visit to the Park!

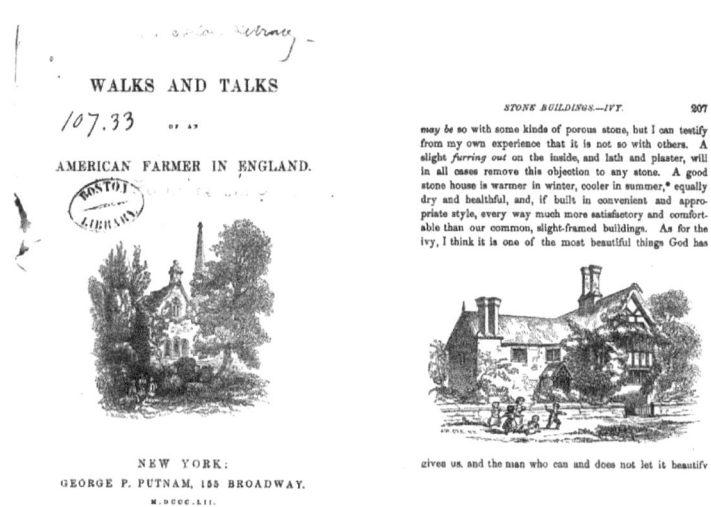

Figs. 43, 44: Illustration from Walks and Talks, *1857 edition*

Fig. 45: Olmsted in working gear, 1857. Image: Wikipedia

CENTRAL PARK: THE EARLY YEARS

4.3 CALVERT VAUX

The next "Founding Father" to appear on the scene was Calvert Vaux (1824-1895, Fig. 48), a British-born landscape architect who had been working in New York since 1851. He had published several books on architecture (Figs. 46, 47).

Vaux came to America as the business partner of Andrew Jackson Downing, America's most prominent landscape designer. Downing soon introduced Vaux to Olmsted. Downing would certainly have been involved with the design of Central Park, had he not died in 1852 in a steamboat accident.

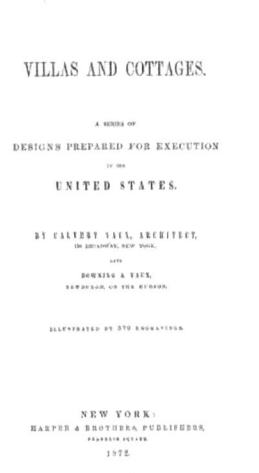

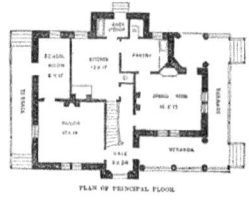
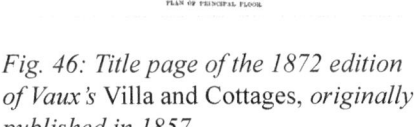

Fig. 46: Title page of the 1872 edition of Vaux's Villa and Cottages, *originally published in 1857*

Fig. 47: From Vaux's Villas and Cottages, *1872 edition*

Fig. 48: Calvert Vaux (1824-1895). Image: Clarence Cook, A Description of the New York Central Park, *1869*

4.4 THE DESIGN COMPETITION

Calvert Vaux condemned Viele's 1856 plan for Central Park as just the sort of mundane design one would expect from an engineer. He said it had "manifest defects" and would be a disgrace to the city and to Downing's memory. Vaux persuaded the Board of Commissioners to sponsor a competition for the Park's design. Their advertisement ran in October 1857 (Fig. 49).

The Board listed a hodgepodge of requirements—a combination of the demands of those who wanted the Park to provide a place for fresh air and exercise, or pastoral views, or culture. For a construction cost of $1.5 million, designs submitted to the Board were to provide:

- Space for a new, larger reservoir.
- At least four transverse roads, to carry commercial traffic across the Park
- A parade ground for military drills
- Three playgrounds
- Possible sites for an exhibition or concert hall, an observatory, a skating pond, and a lookout tower
- Fountains and flower gardens

The Board's advertisement drew <u>thirty-three entries</u> in a wide range of styles. The medal for Least Practical Design goes to John Rink. His formal, symmetrical elements gallop blithely across streams, swamps, and rocky outcrops, from the depressed area at the southwest right up to the rocky hills of the northwest (Fig. 50).

Calvert Vaux recruited Frederick Law Olmsted to create a joint entry. As Park superintendent, Olmsted had boots on the ground—often up to his knees. But so did eleven of the other thirty-two contestants. Among them was Viele, the Park's chief engineer, who resubmitted his 1856 plan.

The winner of the competition was announced in April 1858: Vaux and Olmsted's Greensward Plan.

4.5 THE GREENSWARD PLAN

The ten-foot long Greensward Plan that Olmsted and Vaux drew still exists, but hasn't yet been digitized. Figure 51 is the black-and-white version published by the *New York Times*.

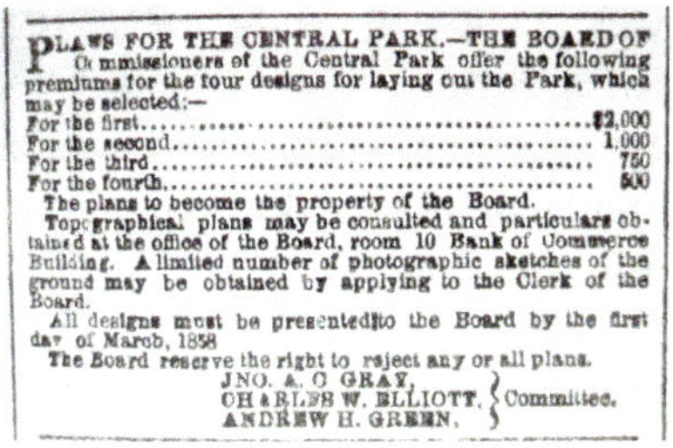

PLANS FOR THE CENTRAL PARK.—THE BOARD OF Commissioners of the Central Park offer the following premiums for the four designs for laying out the Park, which may be selected:—

For the first.......................................$2,000
For the second.......................................1,000
For the third.......................................750
For the fourth.......................................500

The plans to become the property of the Board.

Topographical plans may be consulted and particulars obtained at the office of the Board, room 10 Bank of Commerce Building. A limited number of photographic sketches of the ground may be obtained by applying to the Clerk of the Board.

All designs must be presented to the Board by the first day of March, 1858

The Board reserve the right to reject any or all plans.

JNO. A. C GRAY,
CHARLES W. ELLIOTT, } Committee.
ANDREW H. GREEN,

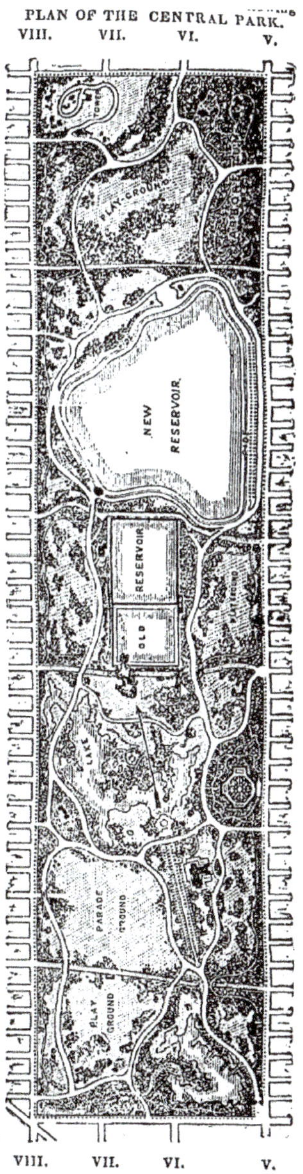

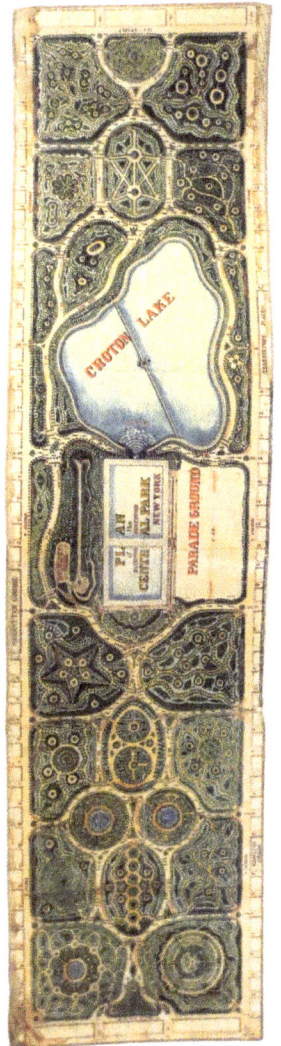

Fig. 49: Advertisement for the competition for the design of Central Park, October 1857

Fig. 50 (upper right): John Rink's entry for the Central Park design competition, 1857 or 1858. Image: New-York Historical Society

Fig. 51 (lower left): The Greensward Plan, as published in the New York Times *on May 1, 1858.*

Olmsted and Vaux's design was a pastoral landscape in the romantic tradition of the Hudson River School painters. (See Chapter 2.3.6.) It was intended to be a sharp contrast to the city's "monotonous straight streets and piles of rectangular buildings," providing picturesque vistas for quiet contemplation. Charming and unexpected views appeared around the corner or at the top of the hill. But as the Board of Commissioners pointed out, the Greensward Plan was not a return to nature: it looked nothing like the way Manhattan would have looked before human settlement.

> If the ... primeval forest [could be] restored, however,—only such walks and drives being constructed through it as would make all parts readily accessible,—the general effect would still be unsatisfactory, from the want of breadth and expanse in the landscapes. It would be—so to speak—monotonous in its irregularity, the eye soon wearying of the ceaseless repetition of rocks and hillocks, with meagre depressions of surface between them. (*Third Annual Report of the Board of Commissioners of the Central Park, January 1860*, p. 37)

The Greensward Plan fell into three sections: south, middle, and north.

The south end of the plan (Fig. 52) was formal, with rolling meadows and carefully constructed views. It included a promenade that had not been required by the Board of Commissioners. "The Mall" is a

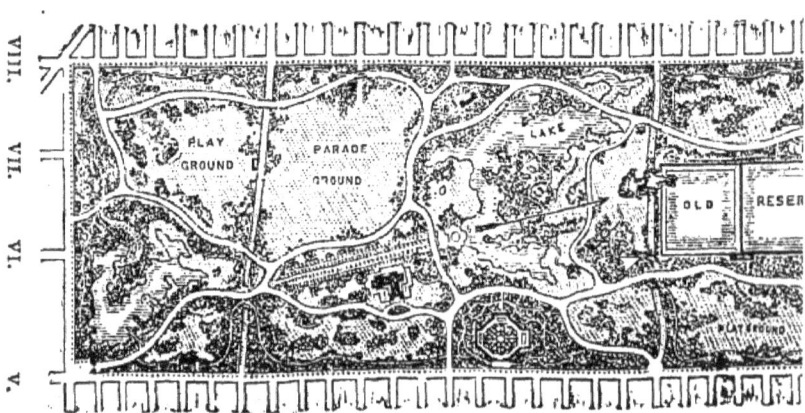

Fig. 52: Greensward Plan, south end, from the 5/1/1858 New York Times. *North is to the right. The Mall is the dotted line just below (east of) the Parade Ground.*

CENTRAL PARK: THE EARLY YEARS

Fig. 53: Rustic shelter in the Ramble. Image: Appleton's, February 8, 1872

Fig. 54: The Mall in Central Park in 1864, looking northeast toward the arbor. Image: W.H. Guild and Frederic B. Perkins, The Central Park, *1864*

Fig. 55: Rustic shelter in the Ramble, 1862. Image: New York Public Library Digital Collections

Fig. 56: South end of Central Park in 1859. North is to the right. The twisting paths of the Ramble are just left (south) of the Old Reservoir. Image: New York Public Library Digital Collections

nod to those who wanted culture in the Park: a public meeting place, where the upper and middle classes could see and be seen. Vaux and Olmsted explained:

> Although averse on general principles to a symmetrical arrangement of trees, we consider it an essential feature of a metropolitan park, that it should contain a grand promenade, level, spacious and thoroughly shaded.

The shade came from four rows of elms, arranged like columns in the nave of a church. In 1864, the adolescent elms were still spindly and adorable (Fig. 54).

The Board of Commissioners' report for 1858 called the Mall a "grand cathedral avenue." The cathedral's apse was Bethesda Terrace, just north of 72nd Street. But Olmsted and Vaux did not want architecture to dominate the Park, so they dropped the "apse" below the level of the Mall, making it accessible via a grand staircase. (See Chapter 6.1.) The view they intended visitors to see from the north end of the Mall is marked on the New York Times map: across the Lake to the Ramble (Fig. 52).

Just north of the Mall is the Lake, placed on the site of a stream and a swamp because Olmsted and Vaux preferred to work with nature rather than fighting it. North of the Lake, on a small hill, is the Ramble. In contrast to the area around the Mall, the Ramble has a rustic feel, with benches and bridges made of unfinished wood (Fig. 53, 55). The paths are narrow and twisting, with short lines of sight. It's designed to encourage ... well, rambling (Fig. 56). This description of the Ramble as it was intended to look over time was probably penned by Olmsted:

> The middle distance [of the landscape view from the Mall will be] composed of rocks, with evergreens and dark shrubs interspersed among them, reflected in the pond [i.e., the Lake]; and the distance extended into intricate obscurity by carefully planting shrubs of lighter and more indistinct foliage among and above the gray rocks of the back-ground. (_Fourth Annual Report of the Board of Commissioners of the Central Park, January 1861,_ p. 116)

North of the Ramble was the original Croton Aqueduct Receiving Reservoir (see Chapter 2.4.4), and then the new reservoir, which stretched nearly the width of the Park.

CENTRAL PARK: THE EARLY YEARS

Above the new reservoir, from 96th to 106th Street, the Greensward Plan called for a less developed area: fewer paths, more natural features, and sweeping views (Fig. 57).

Here's our timeline to date.
- 1853: Purchase of land for Central Park was authorized
- 1857: Last of the land for the Park was paid for
- 1856: Clearing of the land was begun, under Viele
- 1857-1858: Competition was held for the design of Central Park
- 1858, April: Greensward Plan won competition

Now all they had to do was execute the Greensward Plan, right?

It wasn't quite that simple.

Fig. 57: North end of Central Park in 1859, from the new reservoir to 106th Street. Image: New York Public Library Digital Collections

CHAPTER 5
Construction of Central Park

5.1 EXECUTION OF THE GREENSWARD PLAN

A few years after construction began, Olmsted wrote a long letter to Vaux, setting out what he saw as their respective roles in Central Park. He credited the two of them with an equal share in the design of the Greensward Plan. Vaux was responsible for all the architectural design. Olmsted was responsible for managing the construction force and for teaching the public how to use the park. (For Olmsted's 1863 letter to Vaux, see Morrison H. Heckscher, *Creating Central Park,* p. 39.)

Beginning in the summer of 1858, Olmsted, as architect-in-chief, supervised as many as 3,800 laborers per day in the Park. It wasn't easy. Construction jobs in the Park, like most government-controlled jobs at the time, were handed out via the spoils system. If you knew the right guy, you got the job—no matter what your qualifications. Many workers believed it was their right to scam the system, showing up just enough to collect their pay. In an era before punch-clocks and video surveillance, Olmsted devised a way to make sure his men remained on the job all day. He also worked out protocols to guarantee that massive amounts of construction materials were dispatched where needed. Despite having no experience of construction on this scale, he proved to be an extremely competent administrator.

The crews worked from south to north, finishing the Park in about twenty years (Figs. 58, 59). Not a single square yard of the Park's 1.3 square miles remains as it was in 1850. For example: Sheep Meadow (Fig. 60) was imposed on a rocky swamp.

> The boggy portion has been filled in to an average depth of two feet, and all rocks protruding have been removed by blasting; some large ledges of rock adjoining have been reduced, and the intervening depressions filled in a similar manner; all remaining rock surface has then been covered with two feet of soil, and thus about thirty acres of level or but slightly undulating ground has been formed … (*Fourth Annual Report of the Board of Commissioners of the Central Park, January 1861*, p. 114)

CENTRAL PARK: THE EARLY YEARS

Fig. 58: Construction of Central Park, an 1859 Currier & Ives print. Image: New York Public Library Digital Collections

Fig. 59: Construction of Central Park, an 1859 Currier & Ives print. Image: New York Public Library Digital Collections

Fig. 60: Sheep Meadow. Photo copyright © 2013 Dianne L. Durante

The Park was already open for business as workers blasted away rock in the Sheep Meadow and elsewhere with 21,000 barrels of gun powder. Visitors were expected to take care of themselves. The Board of Commissioners posted warning signs:

> Beware of Blasts. The Board of Commissioners of the Central Park will not be responsible for any damage suffered by anyone, in person or property, within the Park, by reason of blasting, or the operations or means of construction of the Park. (copy of the sign is in the New York City Archives)

The workers shifted three or four million cubic yards of stone and dirt. They laid mile after mile of drainage pipes, to keep the swamps and streams under control and to handle run-off after rainstorms. They hauled in 700,000 cubic yards of topsoil and landscaped it with 270,000 trees, shrubs, and flowers. And they did all this with brute muscle: horsepower and manpower.

5.2 EARLY REVISIONS TO THE GREENSWARD PLAN

Even as construction began, major changes were made to the Greensward Plan.

5.2.1 The Extension, 106-110th Streets

At 106th Street, the north end of the Park ended amid very rocky terrain. But at 110th Street, after a steep bluff, the land flattened out to Harlem Heights. The city had assigned itself the task of laying out and cutting all streets according to the 1811 Commissioners' Plan, as the city's population moved ever northward. That ridiculously rocky bit from 106th to 110th Streets ... why not just add it to the Park, so streets didn't have to be cut there?

In 1860, the four blocks of the Extension (Fig. 61) were appraised at $184,000. By 1863, when the land was actually purchased, Central Park was well under way, and the value of land near it was

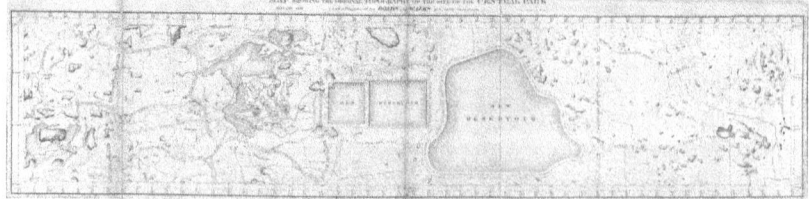

Fig. 61: Map of Central Park, 1859. The Extension begins near the right (north), at the orange loop on the Great Hill. Image: New York Public Library Digital Collections

CENTRAL PARK: THE EARLY YEARS

skyrocketing. The city paid $1.5 million for those four north-south blocks. For the other forty-seven north-south blocks, they had paid only $5 million.

Olmsted and Vaux incorporated the Extension into their design, adding the Loch, the Ravine, and the Harlem Meer. They also let stand a military relic, the only building in the Park that's older than the Arsenal. For two centuries, New York's main defenses were at the Battery, facing the harbor. But during the War of 1812, the British attacked Connecticut. New Yorkers suddenly realized they could be attacked from the north, via Long Island Sound. A series of watchtowers was hastily built in the heights at the north end of Manhattan. They were completed around the time that a peace treaty was signed with Britain.

By the 1860s, only one of the watchtowers remained, around 109th Street. It was known as the "Blockhouse" (Figs. 62, 63). Veterans still remembered it as a military installation, raising flags there on special occasions: July 4th, Evacuation Day (November, 25, 1783, when the British forces sailed away from New York), and January 8, 1815 (the date of Andrew Jackson's victory over the British at the Battle of New Orleans).

Olmsted and Vaux let the Blockhouse stand, but instead of emphasizing its military function, they turned it into a picturesque, vine-covered ruin. (It has since been cleared of vines and its stonework restored.)

Fig. 62: The Blockhouse in the 1860s, with the bluff dropping to 110th Street on the right. Image: New York Public Library Digital Collections

Fig. 63: Harlem Heights, with the Blockhouse at left. Image: Benson John Lossing, The Hudson from the Wilderness to the Sea, *1866*

5.2.2 The Bow Bridge

Olmsted and Vaux, who designed the Park as a pastoral retreat, wanted visitors to take their time strolling around the Lake in order to reach the Ramble. The Board of Commissioners, however, often favored the Park as a meeting place and center of culture. They demanded a shortcut from the Mall to the Ramble. That's why we have the elegant, cast-iron Bow Bridge (Figs. 64, 65).

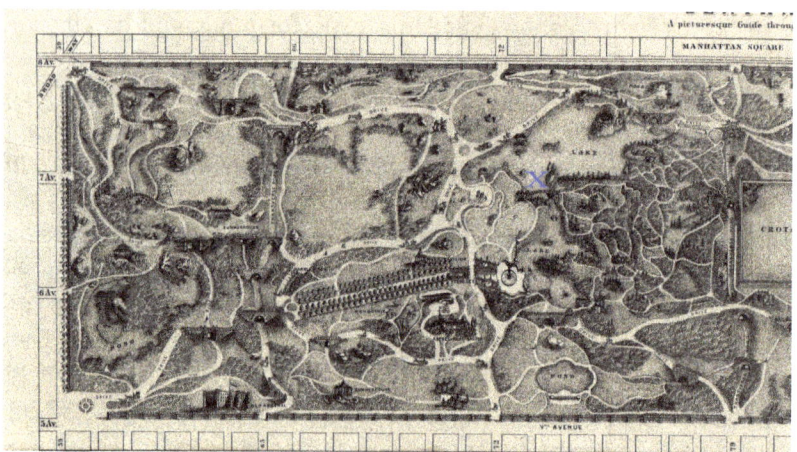

Fig. 64: 1865 map of Central Park. Image: David Rumsey Map Collection. "X" marks the spot of the Bow Bridge, shortening the distance from the Mall to the Ramble.

Fig. 65: The Bow Bridge. Image: W.H. Guild and Frederic B. Perkins, The Central Park, *1864*

5.2.3 The circulation system

The third major change to the Greensward Plan—and the most important one—concerned the roads and paths in the Park. Viele introduced the idea of transverse roads to carry commercial traffic between the east and west sides of the Park. But in Viele's plan, the Park's roads and the transverse roads were at the same level. That meant business and pleasure would collide, with potentially disastrous consequences, at every intersection of the transverse roads with the Park's other paths. Olmsted and Vaux made a major improvement to Viele's idea: they sunk the transverse roads, sending commercial traffic out of sight and out of hearing, and putting Park visitors out of harm's way.

But the other roads in the Greensward Plan were not so well thought out. The Plan called for a carriage drive 60 feet wide—the width of most cross streets in Manhattan. The drive was flanked on either side by a four-foot grass border, and then a six-foot wide walking path.

In 1858, just as construction was getting under way, two members of the Board of Commissioners (one of them August Belmont, for whom the Belmont Stakes are named) insisted on having a bridle path in the Park. Not only that: the bridle path had to be separate from the carriage and pedestrian paths.

> A carriage coming directly upon the course of a pedestrian or of a man on horseback, is often an annoyance, sometimes positively dangerous. ... The mere consciousness that one's path may be crossed by a horse or carriage, causes with some a feeling of anxiety. (*Fourth Annual Report of the Board of Commissioners of the Central Park, January 1861*, p. 117)

All those gorgeous decorative bridges in the south end of the Park were added to the Greensward Plan in order to separate the pedestrians, horseback riders, and carriages (Figs. 66, 67).

Fig. 66: Greywacke Arch, near the Metropolitan Museum. Image: Annual Report of the Board of Commissioners of the Central Park, *1861*

Fig. 67: Bridge No. 28, a.k.a. the "Gothic Bridge, 1863. Image: Annual Report of the Board of Commissioners of the Central Park, *1864. Cast iron was at the time a high-tech material: No. 28, the Bow Bridge, and four other bridges were constructed of it.*

Olmsted and Vaux arranged for visitors emerging from any underpass to have a charming, unexpected view. Thus they turned a demand of the cultural faction into an element of their pastoral park—and at the same time, created a remarkably efficient system of traffic management for the Park's tens of thousands of visitors.

5.3 FINANCES: ANDREW HASWELL GREEN

Andrew Haswell Green (1820-1903, Fig. 68) is most famous as the driving force behind the consolidation of Manhattan, Brooklyn, Queens, the Bronx, and Staten Island into New York City in 1898. But long before that, he was one of Central Park's "Founding Fathers". As a member of the Board of Commissioners from 1857 to 1870, Green was the man largely responsible for managing the massive amount of money expended on Central Park's construction. The memorial bench near the north end of Central Park commemorates both Green's roles (Fig. 69).

As the Park's comptroller, Green minutely questioned every bill submitted by Architect-in-Chief Olmsted. Olmsted bitterly accused Green of a "constitutional reluctance to pay." But even with Green's zeal for curbing costs, the Central Park project ran far over budget.

The design competition in 1858 had limited the construction cost to $1.5 million. (See Chapter 4.4.) In 1859, New York State authorized $2 million for construction of the Park. That disappeared so quickly that in 1860, the state legislature dispatched Julius Kellersberger, a

Fig. 68: Andrew Haswell Green, ca. 1868. Image: Museum of the City of New York

Fig. 69: The Green Bench, dedicated 1920 at the north end of Central Park (near the East Drive at about 103rd St.). Inscription: "1920 In honor of Andrew Haswell Green 1903. / Directing Genius of Central Park in its formative period / Father of Greater New York. This eminence was named Andrew H. Green Hill. / These five symbolical trees were planted and this seat was erected." Photo copyright © 2017 Dianne L. Durante

civil engineer, to investigate how all that the money was being spent. Kellersberger reported that the Park's agricultural drainage was "effectually and satisfactorily executed," the superficial drainage also done "in a systematic and approved manner," the roads "very good and substantial," the bridges "of the most substantial and perfect character," and the system for bringing water for irrigation and fountains "good and economical." He also noted that the management (i.e., Olmsted) had the labor force well in hand:

> The works are carried on under efficient and proper supervision, and under a strict discipline; the best order and system prevails in the different offices as well as on the grounds, and in that respect there is no other public work in the United States to be compared with the Central Park.

Kellersberger concluded:

> I would state, that the plan and laying out of the park, the design, location, and proper construction of the four transverse roads, the division of roads and drives, rides and walks, the availing of natural propensities, the graceful grades and curvatures, the magnificent bridges, beautiful lakes and picturesque landscape, do as much honor to the taste, refinement, and wealth of the metropolis, as credit to its designer and executor. (*Fourth Annual Report of the Board of Commissioners of the Central Park, January 1861*, pp. 120-122)

Seven years into the construction, an additional $3.6 million was needed. By 1877, about $10 million had been invested in the Park.

Due to the efficiency of Olmsted and Green, the New York State legislature allotted more power and larger budgets to the Board of Commissioners of Central Park. Soon the Board was supervising every park in Manhattan. It also controlled major construction projects such as building bridges between Manhattan and the Bronx. And as Manhattan's population grew, the Board authorized and supervised the cutting of streets in accordance with the 1811 Commissioners' Plan. Annually, the Board managed thousands of employees and millions of dollars.

And that put a target on their back. When Boss Tweed and his cronies grabbed control of New York City's government in 1870, they also took control of the Board of Commissioners of Central Park. We'll see the effect of that in Chapter 8. (Spoiler: not good.)

CHAPTER 6
Architectural Elements of Central Park

Vaux and Olmsted's policy was, "Nature first, second, and third—architecture after a while." In the Greensward Plan, they envisioned the Park as a pastoral landscape. Of the structures standing before the land for the Park was purchased, they left in place only the Blockhouse at 109th Street and the Arsenal at Fifth Avenue and 63rd Street ("a very unattractive structure, and only tolerably built"). The Greensward Plan called for some rustic shelters in the Ramble, a restaurant, and a building for the use of children at the playground. But more architectural features were added through the 1870s. We'll concentrate on those still standing. The Mineral Springs, the Music Pavilion, the Casino, and Vaux's Boathouse have all disappeared.

6.1 BETHESDA TERRACE

Bethesda Terrace was completed in the late 1860s (Figs. 70, 71). If the Mall is the nave of a church, the Terrace is the apse—but it's at the level of the Lake, so that it doesn't interrupt the view from the Mall to the Ramble. (See Chapter 4.5.) Bethesda Terrace was designed by Calvert Vaux and Jacob Wrey Mould (Fig. 72). Vaux's original plan

Fig. 70: View from the Lake or the Ramble south to Bethesda Terrace, 1866. The Angel of the Waters *had not yet been put in place. Image: Benson John Lossing,* The Hudson from the Wilderness to the Sea, *1866*

Fig. 71: Bethesda Terrace under construction, 1862. Image: New York Public Library Digital Collections

Fig. 72: Bethesda Terrace, 1862. The man is either Jacob Wrey Mould or the photographer Victor Prevost. Image: Eastman Museum

CENTRAL PARK: THE EARLY YEARS 53

Figs. 73, 74, 75: Decorative elements on Bethesda Terrace. Photos copyright © 2017 Dianne L. Durante

called for twenty bronze sculptures for the steps, but those were never executed. The elaborate decorative program on the piers includes representations of the four seasons and times of day. (Figs. 72, 73, 74, 75.)

The decorative elements here and elsewhere in the Park were mostly the work of Mould. He was also responsible for the Sheepfold (now Tavern on the Green), the Cherry Hill Fountain, the Stables (on the 86th Street Transverse, now home of the Central Park Precinct of the N.Y.P.D.), and the earliest staircases at the Metropolitan Museum (see Chapter 6.7). Mould seems to have been a follower and assistant rather than a leader, except for the brief span in 1870-1871 when Tweed's cronies controlled the Park. So, although his work is lovely, Mould doesn't quite rank as a "Founding Father".

6.2 THE BELVEDERE

The highest point in the southern end of Central Park is Vista Rock, at the southwest corner of the original reservoir, on the 79th Street Transverse. During the construction of Central Park, Vista Rock was topped by a fire tower (Fig. 76).

In the Greensward Plan, Olmsted and Vaux noted that on Vista Rock, "a tower should be erected, but by no means a large one, or the whole scale of the view will be destroyed" (*New York Times* 5/1/1858). Within a few years Vaux designed a castle, named "Belvedere" because it commanded a beautiful view over the Park (Fig. 77). It was perched on the corner of the original reservoir, so that it would be quaintly reflected there (Fig. 78).

As the only artificial structure visible from the north end of the Mall and Bethesda Terrace, the Belvedere was intended to be the focal point of the view (as in Fig. 80). So that it would seem to be grander and further away, Vaux designed it at three-quarter scale (Fig. 79). There isn't room inside for much more than a small gift shop.

The Belvedere is no longer visible from the Mall: not even the flag atop the castle, not even in the dead of winter. Nobody wants to chop down 150-year-old trees in the Ramble, even though they destroy a vista that Olmsted and Vaux considered one of the most important in the Park.

CENTRAL PARK: THE EARLY YEARS

Fig. 76: 79th Street Transverse, with the tunnel blasted through solid rock and the fire tower, ca. 1863-1865. Stairs were cut from near the Belvedere down to the tunnel so that visitors could admire this engineering marvel. The other transverses can only be approached from the east or west side of the Park. Image: New York Public Library Digital Collections

Fig. 77: Bird's-eye view of Central Park from above the Belvedere, 1875. Image: New York Public Library Digital Collections

Fig. 78: The Belvedere reflected in the original reservoir (ca. 1900?). Image: New York Public Library Digital Collections

Fig. 79: The Belvedere, 1870. Image: ArchiMaps (with date 1899)

Fig. 80: View from the north end of the Mall in 1882, showing Bethesda Terrace, the Lake, and the Belvedere. It's copied from an earlier sketch: by this time, the simple fountain on the Terrace had been replaced by the Angel of the Waters.

6.3 THE DAIRY

Did you ever wonder why there's a dairy in Central Park? It was not one of the Board of Commissioners' numerous requirements. (See Chapter 4.4.) Nor was it in the Greensward Plan. The Dairy is the result of a media frenzy.

In May 1858, just after the Greensward Plan won the competition and construction on the Park was beginning, *Frank Leslie's Illustrated Newspaper* began an exposé on swill milk (Fig. 81). In Manhattan, distilleries processed grain to extract alcohol. Then (waste not, want not) they fed what was left of the grain to dairy cows. The cows did not thrive on this diet: the milk they produced was thin, blue, and not very nutritious. In an attempt to make it more attractive, "swill milk" was doctored with flour, plaster of Paris, and other materials. *Leslie's* demanded that the Board of Health shut down the distillery dairies. *Leslie's* reporters were not the first to reveal the hazards of swill milk, but they were the first to publish the facts in a mass-market publication with gruesome illustrations, so their story had an enormous impact.

CENTRAL PARK: THE EARLY YEARS 57

Fig. 81: Frank Leslie's Illustrated Weekly, *May 15, 1858*

Fig. 82: Sketch of the Dairy from Appleton's Magazine, *1872*

Fig. 83: Sketch for the Dairy from the <u>Annual Report of the Board of Commissioners of the Central Park for 1868</u>

It's easy to spin swill milk production as heartless businessmen starving babies. The facts were not that simple. Then as now, children needed milk—but infant formula and canned or powdered milk hadn't yet been invented. New York City was growing rapidly. The areas of not yet developed were unsuitable for grazing, so fresh milk had to be transported in from Brooklyn, New Jersey, or Westchester. In the era before refrigeration and pasteurization, milk transported by ferries and horse-drawn carriages spoiled rapidly. For many Manhattan residents, swill milk was the only milk available. This wider context was not acknowledged by *Leslie's* as it ran article after terror-inducing article on the "distillery dairies".

The Dairy was added to the plan for Central Park quite suddenly, soon after the swill milk exposé in *Leslie's*. Designed by Calvert Vaux in his preferred style, Gothic Revival, it was assigned a spot at the southwest end of the Park, near the children's area (Fig. 82, 83). Its lower level opened onto the 65th Street Transverse, so that horses and carts would not have to trundle through the Park to deliver supplies.

The Dairy was completed under Boss Tweed's reign, around 1870. Since children don't vote, the Dairy opened as a public restaurant. Under Tweed, the uses of the Park that pleased the greatest number of potential voters always won out.

6.4 THE ZOO

From its earliest years, people donated animals to Central Park. In 1873, the Board rejected the gift of an angora goat, because they had been told it smelled "rank". Otherwise, they accepted everything from children's pet dogs to elephants (Figs. 84, 85).

By 1874, when the Park was fifteen years old, it had received six hundred donations. As it turned out, many visitors preferred gazing at animals in the zoo to gazing at the pastoral landscapes so carefully designed by Olmsted and Vaux.

A zoo wasn't part of the original Park plan, and for decades, it was housed in makeshift quarters. Some animals were kept in the basement of the Arsenal, where their stench was a source of continual exasperation to the Board of Commissioners and the park police headquartered above. Other animals were kept in ramshackle cages outdoors, or tethered near the Arsenal (Figs. 86, 87).

The zoo's ramshackle state was so well known that in 1874, the *New York Herald* published a story describing how the animals

From Bayard Clark, presenting a pair of deer for the Park.
On motion of Mr. FIELDS, donation accepted, and communication ordered on file.

From G. Granville White, presenting a male gazelle.
On motion of Mr. FIELDS, donation accepted, and communication ordered on file.

From Bryan Lawrence, presenting the stuffed skins of the mammoth ox "Constitution," and of two large sheep.
On motion of Mr. GREEN, said donations were accepted, and

Animals.
1866.
Jan. 2. One Coatimundi, presented by John Robinson, M. D.
" 5. One Deer, presented by J. Brice, Esq.
" " One Ringtail Monkey, presented by James A. Robertson, Esq.
" 10. One Black Squirrel, presented by Rev. H. H. Messenger.
" 15. One pair Prairie Dogs, } presented by William H. Schieffelin, Esq.
    One Guinea Pig.
" 19. One Young Black Bear, presented by Robert Belloni, Esq.
" 24. One pair Chinese Geese, presented by Captain W. P. Buckhorn.
" 29. One Turkey Buzzard (D.), presented by Jaques Bowman, Esq.
" 31. One Japanese Dog (D.), presented by Arthur S. Hamilton, Esq.
Feb. 2. Two Owls (D.), presented by Messrs. Clark Brothers,
" 3. One pair Box Turtles, presented by Master David Ehrlich.
" 6. One Raccoon, presented by Francis E. Spering, Esq.

Figs. 84, 85: A few of the donations to the Central Park zoo, from the annual reports of the Board of Commissioners of the Central Park, 1863 and 1866

Fig. 86: Central Park Menagerie, 1869. Image: New York Public Library Digital Collections

Fig. 87: Elephant tethered near the Arsenal, 1879. Image: New York Public Library Digital Collections

Fig. 88: Opening of the original hoax, published in the New York Herald, *1874.*

Figs. 89, 90, 91: Cartoons from an 1893 Harper's Weekly *article on the Herald Hoax; more here*

Fig. 92: Jacob Wrey Mould's building for the zoo, usually referred to at this period as the "Menagerie", 1871. Image: New York Public Library Digital Collections

CENTRAL PARK: THE EARLY YEARS

broke free and rampaged through Manhattan. It was one of the most famous media hoaxes of the nineteenth century (Figs. 88, 89, 90, 91).

Boss Tweed and his associates loved construction projects, because they provided opportunities for raking in money via inflated bills and kickbacks. While the Boss controlled the city, he and his cronies ordered Jacob Wrey Mould to design a large wooden building to house some of the animals (Fig. 92). It was completed around 1870, and stood near the Arsenal until Robert Moses renovated the zoo in the 1930s.

6.5 THE SHEEPFOLD

The second building erected while Tweed controlled the Park is still standing. Around 1870, Central Park had some two hundred sheep to enhance the pastoral atmosphere. They grazed in the Sheep Meadow, under the watchful eye of a shepherd (Fig. 93). Visitors were in no danger of stepping on sheep pats, because visitors were not supposed to be strolling on the grass. As Andrew Haswell Green, the financial genius of the Board of Commissioners, explained: "The blades of grass that united, make up a lawn, can be enjoyed without pressing them underfoot."

Fig. 93: Central Park's shepherd. Image: Clarence Cook, A Description of the New York Central Park, *1869*

Fig. 94: Sheepfold, ca. 1870. Image: Wikipedia

Figs. 95, 96: Exterior today, and one of two sheep's heads flanking the fireplace of the Sheepfold. Photos copyright © 2017 Dianne L. Durante

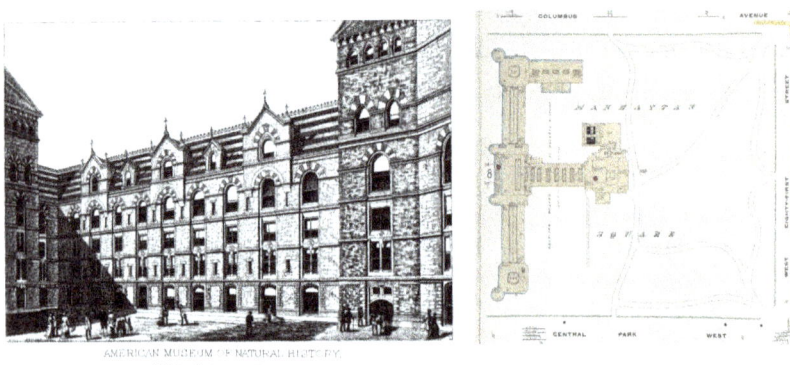

Fig. 97: Part of the paleontological collection at the Arsenal, 1868. Benjamin Waterhouse Hawkins was paid to assemble the dinosaur bones. Image: Wikipedia

Fig. 98: The original part of the American Museum of Natural History, from the annual report of the Board of Commissioners of the Central Park, 1872-1873.

Fig. 99: American Museum of Natural History in 1912. The original Calvert and Vaux building is the small black rectangle just below the "MANH" in "Manhattan Square." Image: New York Public Library Digital Collections

The sheep spent nights in unobtrusive sheds near the reservoir until Boss Tweed and his cronies ordered Jacob Wrey Mould to design a home for them (Figs. 94, 95, 96). It was constructed on the west side of the Park, on a highly visible site at the edge of Sheep Meadow.

After Tweed was thrown into jail in 1871, the Park's engineer reported that the very expensive new Sheepfold was damp, lightless, and unventilated: completely unsuitable for an ovine abode. Andrew Haswell Green suggested turning it into an aquarium. Olmsted argued that it ruined the pastoral view across the Sheep Meadow, and ought to be razed immediately. In the 1930s Robert Moses—a champion of the Park as a place for recreation—turned the Sheepfold into the Tavern on the Green restaurant.

6.6 THE AMERICAN MUSEUM OF NATURAL HISTORY

Two more buildings were added to the Park because Andrew Haswell Green wanted the Park to be a cultural center as well as a pastoral retreat. Central Park routinely received donations not only of live animals, but of stuffed animals, sculptures, dinosaur bones, and other oddments (Fig. 97). In the Park's early years, all these shared space in the Arsenal with live animals, the Board of Commissioners, and the park police.

In 1869, when the Park was about ten years old, the Board of Commissioners authorized the construction of an art museum and a natural history museum. The American Museum of Natural History was assigned a plot of land that had been slated for a park in the Commissioners' Plan of 1811, and was coincidentally adjacent to Central Park. The first section of the building—now buried under added wings and extensions—was designed by Calvert Vaux and Jacob Wrey Mould (Figs. 98, 99). It opened in 1877.

6.7 THE METROPOLITAN MUSEUM OF ART

The other institution given a home in Central Park was the Metropolitan Museum, established by private citizens in 1869. The Board of Commissioners assigned the museum an out-of-the-way space between Fifth Avenue and the old reservoir, and between the 79th and 86th Street Transverses. They envisioned the museum eventually filling up the whole area. But like the American Museum of Natural History, it started small (Figs. 100, 101, 105; compare Fig. 106).

The first wing of the Metropolitan Museum, designed by Vaux and Mould, opened in 1880. Its center is the arched room where the

Christmas tree is now displayed (Galleries 304-305; Fig. 103). The striped arches of the original exterior are still visible from the Lehman Wing and in the second-floor gallery of prints and drawings (Figs. 101, 102). The east end of the original wing is marked by Mould's staircases (Fig. 104).

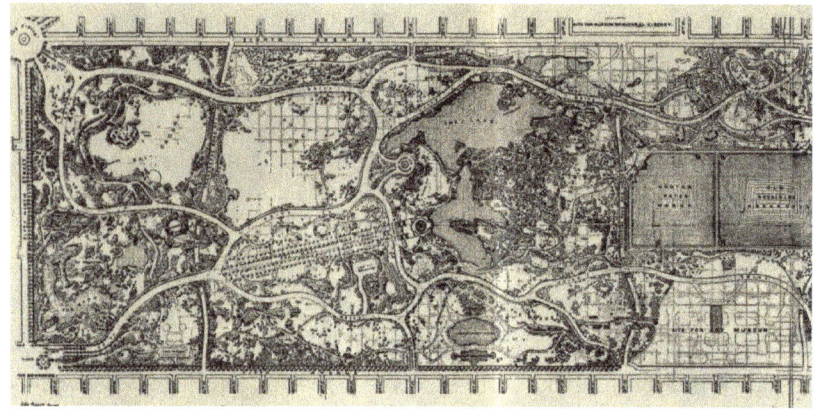

Fig. 100: Southern end of Central Park in 1873. The original wing of the Metropolitan Museum is in gray, in the space at the lower right. Proposed extensions, lightly outlined, fill the rest of the area. Image: Winifred E. Howe, A History of the Metropolitan Museum, *1913*

Fig. 101: The original home (Wing A) of the Metropolitan Museum, ca. 1880. Image: Winifred Howe, A History of the Metropolitan Museum, *1913*

Fig. 102: Section of the west end of the original wing of the Metropolitan Museum, from the Lehman Wing. Photo copyright © 2017 Dianne L. Durante

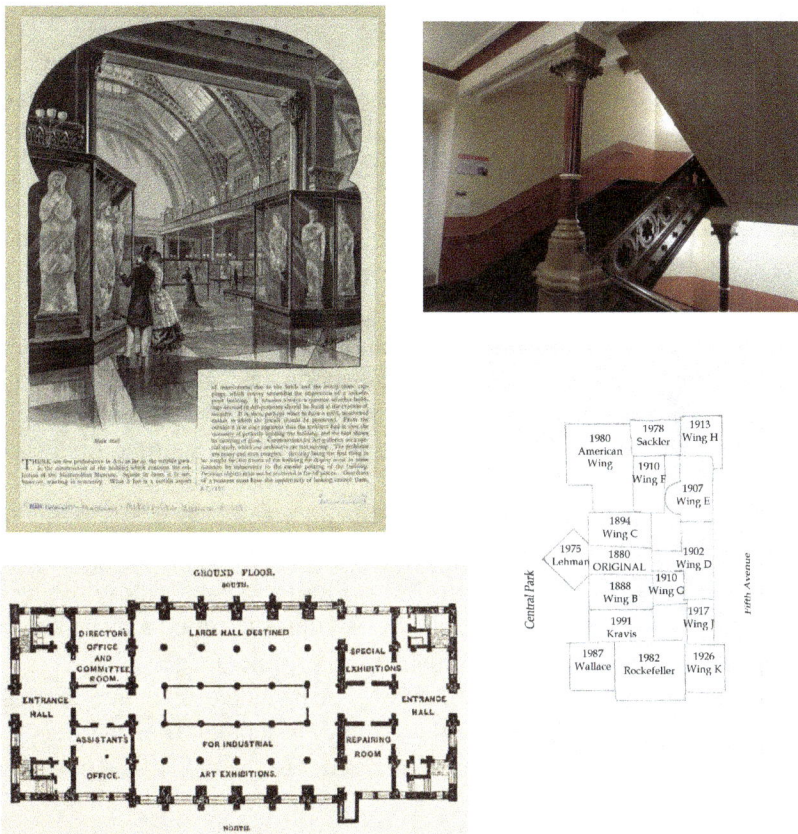

Fig. 103: Original interior of the Metropolitan Museum, 1880. Image: New York Public Library Digital Collections

Fig. 104: One of Mould's staircases from the original wing of the Metropolitan Museum. Photo copyright © 2017 Dianne L. Durante.

Fig. 105: Map of the ground floor of the Metropolitan Museum. The surviving Mould staircases are those flanking the Entrance Hall, at the right. Image: Winifred E. Howe, A History of the Metropolitan Museum, *1913*

Fig.106: Sketch of the expansion of the Metropolitan Museum through 1991. Sketch copyright © 2016 Dianne L. Durante. More on ForgottenDelights.com.

6.8 WALL AND GATES

The last major architectural features of the Park that we'll look at are the wall and gates around its six-mile perimeter. The Greensward Plan called for a row of trees and a four-foot-high wall at the edge of the Park—but even such a simple enclosure was difficult. Outcrops, hills, and valleys contributed to the pastoral effect within the Park, but at the Park's edges, the land had to be blasted or filled so the streets and sidewalks around the Park were more or less level. Once that was done, thousands of tons of stone blocks were quarried, hauled to Manhattan, shaped, set into place, and chiseled into uniformity. In 1863, the Board of Commissioners ordered work on the wall to begin. It took more than a decade to complete. That's part of the reason that if you walk around the Park's perimeter, you'll see so many different colors of stone and different styles of chisel marks.

And then there was the question of the entrances to the Park. If those who favored culture had their way, the gates would have been huge and elaborate, like those of European parks. With those models in mind, noted architect Richard Morris Hunt submitted a remarkable plan for the main entrance, at the southeast corner (Fig. 107).

In the end, the Board of Commissioners voted to create simple entrances—gaps in the wall—that would be named after the people who used the Park. The names are carved into the wall at the sides of the entrances (Fig. 108).

Fig. 107: Richard Morris Hunt's 1866 plan for the southeast entrance of Central Park, near the Plaza Hotel and the Pond. Image: Hunt, Designs for the Gateways of the Southern Entrances to the Central Park, *1866*

CENTRAL PARK: THE EARLY YEARS

When the Park was five years old, Andrew Haswell Green wrote a lengthy essay on the choice of names for the gates. It is also a reminder of the original reasons for building the Park.

> The construction of the Park has been easily achieved, because the industrious population of New York has been wise enough to require it, and rich enough to pay for it: to New Yorkers it belongs wholly, and these four principal gateways may, perhaps, be allowed to recognize this proprietary right, and to extend to each citizen a respectful welcome.
>
> It should, however, be remembered in this connection, that while the Park is intended as a place for freedom and relaxation, for play, and not for work, it has been constructed with no idea of encouraging habits of laziness, or in any way for the benefit of idlers and drones; it is an extensive pleasure-ground, planted conveniently in our midst, so that innocent recreation may quickly follow peaceful labor, and its paramount object is to offer facilities for a daily enjoyment of life to the industrious thousands who are working steadily and conscientiously in the great city which spreads in every direction around it.
>
> The pervading sentiment embodied both in its original conception and in all the details that appertain to its actual execution, may, in fact, be briefly expressed in the three words, "Pleasure with Business;' or, for the sake of still further generalizing the whole idea, we may take the nobler words, "Beauty with Duty."
>
> If an attempt is made to analyze the various industrial pursuits of a large city like New York, it will be found that they

Fig. 108: The Merchants' Gate, at Columbus Circle (59th Street, Central Park West, and Broadway). Photo copyright © 2017 Dianne L. Durante

may be easily grouped under a few leading heads. ... (Fifth Annual Report of the Board of Commissioners of the Central Park, 1862, pp. 125-136)

Around the Park, the gates are as follow.
- Central Park South, east to west: Scholars', Artists', Artisans', Merchants'
- Central Park West, south to north: Merchants', Womens', Hunters', Mariners', All Saints, Boys', Strangers'
- Central Park North, west to east: Warriors', Farmers', Pioneers'
- Fifth Avenue, north to south: Pioneers', Girls', Woodman's, Engineers', Miners', Inventors', Childrens', Scholars'

CHAPTER 7
Sculptures in Central Park

7.1 EARLIEST SCULPTURES

7.1.1 Bethesda Fountain, dedicated 1873

The only sculpture Olmsted and Vaux called for in the Greensward Plan was for the fountain at the center of Bethesda Terrace. In 1863, the commission for the fountain was given to Emma Stebbins (1815-1882), an American-born sculptor working in Rome who was the sister of a member of the Board of Commissioners.

Stebbins's eight-foot-tall fountain figure is an allegory for the life-saving, clean water of the Croton Aqueduct. According to Scripture (John 5:2-4), at Bethesda, near Jerusalem, an angel occasionally came down to stir the waters of a certain pool. The first person to step into the pool afterwards was cured of anything that ailed him. The main figure of Bethesda Fountain is the Angel of the Waters, about to stir (Fig. 110). The four-foot-tall putti below her represent Purity, Health, Temperance, and Peace (Fig. 111). Stebbins sent the sculptures to be cast in 1867, but due to the Franco-Prussian War and a delay in completing the monumental stone basin in Central Park, the fountain was not dedicated until 1873 (Fig. 109).

The *New York Times* (6/1/1873) was scathing about the newly unveiled *Angel of the Waters*. After describing a lovely spring day with children frolicking and a band playing, the *Times* reported:

> When the authorities, without any speech-making or declamation, withdrew the cloakings that shadowed the expected form of art, there was a positive thrill of disappointment. All had expected something great, something of angelic power and beauty, and when a feebly-pretty idealess thing of bronze was revealed, the revulsion of feeling was painful.

But familiarity often breeds fondness: it's difficult to imagine anything else topping the fountain at Bethesda Terrace.

Aside from animals—live, stuffed, fossilized (see Chapter 6.4 and 6.6)—people also donated art to Central Park. Much of it was stored

Fig. 109: Bethesda Terrace in 1875, with peacocks on the loose

Fig. 110: Emma Stebbins, Bethesda Fountain, *dedicated 1873. Photo copyright © 2017 Dianne L. Durante*

Fig. 111: Emma Stebbins, Bethesda Fountain *putti: three of the four. We know they represent Purity, Health, Temperance, and Peace, but it's not clear which is which. Photo copyright © 2017 Dianne L. Durante*

in the Arsenal, but while Bethesda Fountain was in progress, a number of other sculptures were set outdoors in the Park.

7.1.2 Schiller, 1859, by C.L. Richter

Aside from animals—live, stuffed, fossilized—people also donated art to Central Park, much of which was stored in the Arsenal. The earliest piece to be displayed outdoors was a bronze bust of Johann Christoph Friedrich von Schiller (1759-1805), German playwright and poet. Beethoven based the final movement of the Ninth Symphony on Schiller's "Ode to Joy"; Donizetti, Rossini, and Verdi all composed operas inspired by Schiller's plays. Olmsted stashed *Schiller* in the Ramble, to keep him from disrupting the pastoral vibe elsewhere (Fig. 112). The bust is now on the Mall, near Beethoven and opposite the Naumburg Bandshell.

7.1.3 Eagles and Prey, dedicated 1863, by Christophe Fratin

Cast in 1850, *Eagles and Prey* (Fig. 113) is the oldest sculpture in the Park—unless you consider the Obelisk a sculpture. (*Schiller* was cast later than *Eagles* but dedicated earlier.) Christophe Fratin was a member of the "animalier" school that flourished during the mid-nineteenth century. The animaliers specialized in the naturalistic representation of animals with a romantic slant: animals displaying emotions that humans could relate to. This sculpture of eagles ripping apart a goat probably had a more immediate meaning for the Board of Commissioners. When construction of the Park began, the many goats

Fig. 112: C.L. Richter, Schiller, *dedicated 1859, shown in the Ramble during the 1860s or 1870s. Image: New York Public Library Digital Collections*

Fig. 113: Christophe Fratin, Eagles and Prey, *1850, dedicated 1863. Photo copyright © 2017 Dianne L. Durante*

wandering free in Manhattan treated the tender new plants as a buffet. At Olmsted's suggestion, the Board offered a dollar (about half a day's wages) to anyone who brought a goat to the pound.

7.1.4 Tigress with Cubs, 1866, by Auguste Cain

This example of animalier sculpture—a tigress bringing a dead peacock to feed her cubs (Fig. 114)—is also an insider's joke. It was originally placed on Cherry Hill, just west of Bethesda Terrace, where live peacocks roamed.

Clarence Cook's 1869 guidebook to Central Park condemned both *Eagles* and *Tigress* as inappropriate to the Park:

> They are, both of them, fine and spirited works of their kind, but they are much better suited to a zoological garden than to a place like the Park, for the ideas they inspire do not belong to the tranquil, rural beauty of the Park scenery. ... They are simply records of carnage and rapine, and however masterly the execution, or however profound the scientific observation they display, they are apart from the purpose of noble art, whose aim is to lift the spirit of man to a higher region and feed him with grander thoughts. (*A Description of the New York Central Park*, p. 73)

Fig. 114: Auguste Cain, Tigress with Cubs, *1866. Central Park Zoo. Photo copyright © 2017 Dianne L. Durante*

Fig. 115: John Quincy Adams Ward, Indian Hunter, *cast 1866, dedicated 1869. Photo copyright © 2017 Dianne L. Durante*

7.1.5 Indian Hunter, dedicated 1869, by John Quincy Adams Ward

Indian Hunter (Fig. 115) was the breakthrough work for John Quincy Adams Ward, who became one of America's leading sculptors. By the 1860s, few New Yorkers had ever seen an Indian: the frontier was two thousand miles to the west. The small model of this sculpture that Ward exhibited in 1865 (now at the Metropolitan Museum) had decidedly Caucasian features. After August Belmont, Richard Morris Hunt, and others commissioned Ward to create a life-size version of *Indian Hunter* for the Park, Ward traveled to the Dakota Territory to study Indians, so that he could render the facial bone structure more accurately.

7.1.6 Seventh Regiment Memorial, dedicated 1869, by John Quincy Adams Ward

In 1867, the Seventh Regiment (also known as the "Silk Stocking Brigade," because it was composed of wealthy New Yorkers) requested permission to erect a memorial to its fifty-eight members who had died during the Civil War (Fig. 116). Although Ward created a figure that looks ordinary, this memorial was the first of its kind: it represented

Fig. 116: John Quincy Adams Ward, Seventh Regiment Memorial, *dedicated 1869. Photo copyright © 2017 Dianne L. Durante*

Fig. 117: Gustaf Blaeser, Alexander von Humboldt, *dedicated 1869. Photo copyright © 2017 Dianne L. Durante*

not a military leader but a citizen-soldier. Towns across the United States commissioned mass-produced variations of the *Seventh Regiment Memorial*.

7.1.7 Humboldt, dedicated 1869, by Gustaf Blaeser

Alexander von Humboldt (1769-1859) was one of those rare men equally fascinated by the trees and the forest. He collected masses of quantitative data, but also wrote the five-volume *Cosmos*, an attempt to integrate all man's knowledge. *Cosmos* was one of the most widely read science books ever written, and may have influenced the decorative scheme for Bethesda Terrace. This bust (Fig. 117) was originally at the Scholar's Gate (Fifth Avenue at Central Park South). It was later moved to face the American Museum of Natural History.

7.1.8 Morse, dedicated 1871, by Byron M. Pickett

In the 1830s, Samuel Finley Breese Morse (1791-1872), a portrait painter and professor at New York University, cobbled together a battery and a single transmission wire and developed what we know as "Morse code". Morse's telegraph made him a wealthy man—and gave the world, for the first time, long-distance communication that was

Fig. 118: Byron M. Pickett, Samuel F.B. Morse, *dedicated 1871. Photo copyright © 2017 Dianne L. Durante*

Fig. 119: Sir John Steell, Sir Walter Scott, *dedicated 1871. Photo copyright © 2017 Dianne L. Durante*

cheap and almost instantaneous. Near-instantaneous transmission of financial data and transactions made regional stock markets in Philadelphia and Boston obsolete. Hence New York's Wall Street became the nation's financial capital (see Chapter 2.2.4). Morse was a hero worldwide, but especially in New York. In June 1871, eighty-year-old Morse became the last man ever to attend the dedication of his own portrait sculpture in Central Park (Fig. 118).

7.1.9 Scott, dedicated 1871, by Sir John Steell

Sir Walter Scott (1771-1832) declined an invitation to be poet laureate of Great Britain in order to create (anonymously) a new genre: the historical novel. From *Waverly* to the *Bride of Lammermoor,* from *Ivanhoe* to *Rob Roy,* Scott's works were enduring bestsellers. On the centennial of Scott's birth, New Yorkers dedicated a sculpture to him in Central Park (Fig. 119).

7.1.10 Shakespeare, dedicated 1872, by John Quincy Adams Ward

During the mid-nineteenth century, the works of William Shakespeare (1564-1616) were being read by fur traders in Wyoming and miners rushing to the California gold fields. In 1864, although the nation was in the throes of civil war, many New Yorkers were eager to commemorate the three-hundredth anniversary of William Shakespeare's birth. The cornerstone for a figure of Shakespeare in Central Park was laid that year (Fig. 120). To raise money for

Fig. 120: Laying the corner of the Shakespeare *pedestal in Central Park, 1864. Image: Harper's Weekly*

Fig. 121: John Quincy Adams Ward, Shakespeare, *dedicated 1872. Photo copyright © 2017 Dianne L. Durante*

the sculpture, Edwin Booth and his brothers Junius Booth and John Wilkes Booth (the future presidential assassin) appeared on stage together for the first and only time, in Shakespeare's *Julius Caesar*. The statue was finally dedicated in 1872 (Fig. 121).

7.1.11 Falconer, dedicated 1875, by George Blackall Simonds

New Yorker George Kemp made much of his fortune selling "Florida Water," advertised as toilet water, aftershave, and relief for insect bites and frayed nerves. You can still buy it today. On a trip to Europe, Kemp fell in love with this sculpture of a young aristocrat flying a falcon, and offered to pay for a copy to stand in Central Park. *Falconer* was set in place high on a rock overlooking the Lake (Fig. 122). The *New York Times* complained that it "should most certainly have been placed at least 15 feet lower than it is," but also commended the *Falconer* as "one of the few really artistic statues that have been placed in Central Park."

7.2 THE BOARD OF COMMISSIONERS' RULES ON SCULPTURE, 1873

When *Angel of the Waters* was dedicated in 1873, so many sculptures were being donated to the Park that the Board of Commissioners decided to set rules for sculptures placed there.

- The Board had to see either a complete sculpture or a finished model before it would authorize placement in the Park.
- The sculpture had to be approved by the presidents of the National Academy of Design, the Metropolitan Museum of Art, and the American Institute of Architects.
- On the Mall, only sculptures commemorating men and events of "far-reaching and permanent interest" could be erected.
- Near each gate, portraits or commemorative sculptures appropriate to that gate could be erected. For example, a sculpture of a woman might be placed near the Women's Gate, or a sculpture of a soldier near the Warriors' Gate.
- No portrait sculpture could be erected until at least five years after its subject had died. That's why Morse was the last person to attend the dedication of his own portrait sculpture (see Chapter 7.1.8).
- Beautiful, dramatic, or poetic sculptures could be placed elsewhere (not in the Mall or at the Gates) *only* if they did not

CENTRAL PARK: THE EARLY YEARS 77

dominate the landscape. Hence the *Falconer* (Fig. 122) sits high on a rock overlooking Terrace Drive (72nd Street).

7.3 THE HALLECK FIASCO, 1877

You've probably never heard of Fitz-Green Halleck, but in the mid-nineteenth century he was among the most famous American-born

Fig. 122: George Blackall Simonds, Falconer, *dedicated 1875. Photo copyright © 2017 Dianne L. Durante*

Fig. 123: James Wilson Alexander MacDonald, Fitz-Greene Halleck, *1877. Photo copyright © 2017 Dianne L. Durante*

Fig. 124: Dedication of the Halleck *sculpture, 1877. Image: New York Public Library Digital Collections*

poets. One of his best-known works is a poem addressed to his recently deceased friend Joseph Rodman Drake:

> Green be the turf above thee,
> Friend of my better days!
> None knew thee but to love thee,
> Nor named thee but to praise ... (more here)

After Halleck died in 1867, William Cullen Bryant, Samuel Morse, Andrew Haswell Green and others asked the Board of Commissioners of Central Park to allow them to erect a sculpture of Halleck on the Mall. Sir Walter Scott and William Shakespeare were already represented. Wasn't it time to add an American writer? The Board approved the request (Fig. 123).

The trouble began in 1877, when the sculpture had been set in place and was ready to be dedicated. Without asking the Board's permission, the donors invited Rutherford B. Hayes, who had just been inaugurated nineteenth president of the United States, to the unveiling. The donors requested that several hundred members of the Seventh Regiment escort President Hayes into the Park. They sent out more than two thousand invitations to New Yorkers prominent in politics, the arts, the military, society, and business.

In 1877, the closest most Americans got to the president was an illustration on a campaign poster, or a picture in a book or newspaper. The Halleck dedication was like today's red-carpet events. Ten thousand people crowded into the Park to get a glimpse of the famous guests (Fig. 124). Once in the Park, they trampled the greenery and hauled off armfuls of spring flowers. The Park police smiled benignly: they thought that this day was an exception to the rules against mauling the greenery.

Olmsted was furious. In a report to the Board in 1877, he noted that almost ten million dollars had been spent on the Park. The value of the Park, said Olmsted, is in its natural elements: if those are destroyed, then we lose the value of the artificial elements such as the bridges and the roads.

> A much higher degree of beauty and poetic influence would be possible but for the necessity of taking so much space for that which in itself is not only prosaic but often dreary and incongruous, that is to say the necessary standing and moving room for the visitors. (Olmsted, *Minutes of the Board of Commissioners for May 1877 to April 1878,* pp. 43-48)

This is the ultimate in advocating the pastoral aspect: the Park would be a lot better if we didn't have to allow the public in!

After the Halleck fiasco in 1877, the Board banned any large gatherings in the Park. The prohibition held until the 1970s, when the city invited pop stars such as Barbra Streisand and Simon and Garfunkel to perform there. The concerts drew more than a hundred thousand spectators—and devastated the Park's grassy areas. But with the city floundering financially, drawing people into the Park and the City was considered more important than preserving the Park.

But that's another story: let's return to the 1870s.

CHAPTER 8
The Tweed Years (1870-1871) and Their Effects

8.1 BOSS TWEED AND HIS CRONIES

By 1870, most of the Park had been completed. But just at that point came a glitch no one had foreseen: Boss Tweed (Figs. 125, 126).

William Magear Tweed (1823-1878) worked his way up from controlling a small district in Manhattan to controlling New York State. By 1870, he was in cahoots with or controlled the mayor of New York, several levels of the judiciary, and most of the New York State legislature.

Thomas Nast, who made his reputation lampooning Tweed, summed Tweed up with the motto, "Let Us Prey" (Fig. 127). Tweed and his cronies stole millions from the city. A sample of their methods:

- The "Tweed Courthouse," on the south side of Chambers Street. In 1858, the year construction began on Central Park, Tweed finagled the state legislature into allotting funds for

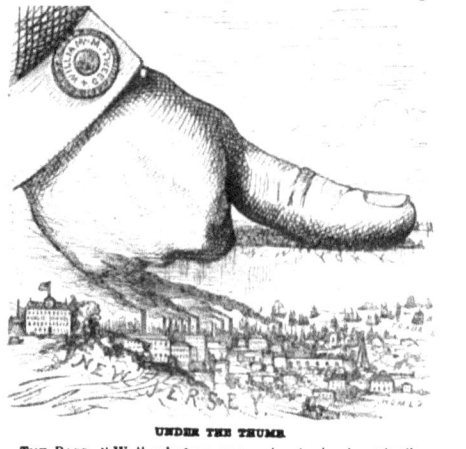

Fig. 125: Thomas Nast: New York under Tweed's thumb. "Well, what are you going to do about it?" Image: Albert Bigelow Paine, Thomas Nast: His Period and His Pictures, *1904, p. 164*

Fig. 126: Boss Tweed, undated photo. Image: Library of Congress

CENTRAL PARK: THE EARLY YEARS

Fig. 127: Thomas Nast's "Let us prey" cartoon. "A group of vultures waiting for the storm to 'blow over.' 'Let us prey.'" The bones Tweed and his cronies have picked over include New York, the New York City treasury, the rent payer, justice, and law. Image: Albert Bigelow Paine, Thomas Nast: His Period and His Pictures, *1904, p. 185*

A GROUP OF VULTURES WAITING FOR THE STORM TO " BLOW OVER."—" LET US *PREY*"

a new city courthouse. Asking for more money became an annual event. By 1871, with the courthouse still unfinished, the cost had skyrocketed to $6.5 million: *twenty-five times* the original estimate.

- Construction kickbacks. Anyone who had a city contract paid an extra 15% to Tweed and his friends. That included construction jobs such as the Sheepfold and the new zoo building in Central Park (see Chapter 6.4, 6.5).
- Salary kickbacks. Teachers paid $75 per year to get a job that paid $300 per year.
- Inflated bills. A friend of Tweed's who was a plasterer was paid $133,000 for two days' work—at a time when a teacher was making something less than $1 per day.
- Rainy-day painting (my personal favorite!). Tweed sent out men to paint lampposts just as it was beginning to rain. The rain washed off the paint, the city had to pay for the job to be done over, and Tweed took another cut.

Tweed's brief reign (1870-1871) did long-lasting financial damage to New York City. He and his cronies collected massive amounts by selling city bonds. They found willing lenders because cities never go bankrupt ... do they? In 1869, New York City's debt was $36 million. In 1870, it was $97 million. By one estimate, Tweed and his cronies made off with about $30 million in cash and about $200 million total. In late 1871 Tweed was arrested, tried, and jailed. The city recovered about $1 million (Fig. 128).

Fig. 128: Thomas Nast, The Tammany Ring: "'Who stole the people's money?' – Do tell. N.Y. Times. 'Twas Him.'" (Tweed is at the left, with his three-carat diamond stud in his cravat.) Image: Albert Bigelow Paine, Thomas Nast: His Period and His Pictures*, 1904, p. 180*

8.2 THE EFFECTS OF TWEED'S REIGN

After Tweed's arrest, New York City couldn't pay even the interest on its debts, never mind the principal. The city's coffers were bare. Andrew Haswell Green, who had been Central Park's financial whiz, was appointed the city's comptroller. To keep the police department and the fire department at work, he borrowed half a million dollars (an enormous sum) on his own responsibility.

As the city's finances tightened, funds for the Park's maintenance were steadily reduced. In the 1860s, $250,000 had been allotted for maintenance of Central Park. In the 1870s, only $100,000 was allotted, and that was for Central Park plus twenty-three other city parks. At one point in the late nineteenth century, maintenance had been neglected so much that only one of the four transverse roads was passable.

Central Park remained in poor condition until the 1930s, when Robert Moses revamped it with millions of dollars in Works Progress Administration money from the federal government. Moses favored the Park as a place for active recreation. On the site of the old reservoir, just west of the Metropolitan Museum, he ordered baseball fields to be constructed. Around the perimeter of the Park, he had twenty playgrounds built.

When the Great Depression ended, massive federal aid to the city also ceased. New York City had to maintain the huge public works that Moses had constructed with far less federal assistance. In addition, during the 1950s and 1960s many New Yorkers fled the deteriorating city to the suburbs, so the city's tax revenues shrunk. By the 1970s, the budget for Central Park had been cut drastically, and the Park suffered (Fig. 129; compare Fig. 130).

The turning point for Central Park was the establishment in 1980 of the Central Park Conservancy, which works in partnership with New York City. The Conservancy is still fighting to balance the Park as a pastoral retreat and as a place for recreation and cultural activities. They do a terrific job. If you enjoy the Park and want to keep enjoying it, why not give them a donation?

Fig. 129: Southeast Reservoir Bridge in the 1960s. Image: Library of Congress.

Fig.130: Southeast Reservoir Bridge today. Photo copyright © 2017 Dianne L. Durante

CHAPTER 9
Episodes in the Forthcoming Guides Who Know Central Park Videoguide

The text of some of these episodes is on DianneDuranteWriter.com: click on "Central Park" in the Obsesssions cloud. When the full app is available, there will be a notice on those pages.

In a series of 75 short videos, the Guides Who Know app on Central Park explores dozens of the Park's most prominent landscape features, buildings, and sculptures. Each three-to seven-minute video offers a lavish number of current photos, archival images, maps, and animations. Orchestral music composed just for this app sets the mood. GPS tells you which sculptures are nearby. CitiMapper tells you how to reach them. Although the app was conceived for visitors to Central Park, you can be entertained and inspired anywhere, anytime.

ANIMALS

Balto, Bears, Eagles and Prey, Falconer, Still Hunt, Tigress

ARCHITECTURE & LANDSCAPE ARCHITECTURE

Arsenal, Belvedere, Bethesda Terrace, Blockhouse, Bridges, Carousel, Dairy, Delacorte Theater, Dene Shelter, Gates, Green Bench, Ladies' Pavilion, Lake, Metropolitan Museum of Art, Obelisk, Ramble, Reservoir / Great Lawn, Sheepfold

CHILDREN

Alice in Wonderland, Andersen, Burnett Memorial, Delacorte Clock, Honey Bear / Dancing Goat, Lehman Zoo Gate, Loeb Fountain, Mother Goose, Osborn Gates, Snow Babies

THE ARTS

Ludwig von Beethoven, Robert Burns, Duke Ellington, Fitz-Green Halleck, Victor Herbert, Richard Morris Hunt, Imagine (John Lennon), Indian Hunter, Thomas Moore, Friedrich Schiller, Sir Walter Scott, William Shakespeare, Bertel Thorvaldsen, Untermyer Fountain

EXPLORERS, SCIENTISTS, INVENTORS

Columbus Monument, Christopher Columbus by Sunol, Alexander von Humboldt, Samuel F.B. Morse, the Pilgrim, Dr. J. Marion Sims

MEDIA

Arthur Brisbane, Joseph Pulitzer, William Stead

POLITICIANS

Frederick Douglass, Alexander Hamilton, Giuseppe Mazzini, Mitchel Memorial, Theodore Roosevelt, Daniel Webster

MILITARY

107th Infantry Memorial, Simon Bolivar, Jagiello, Maine Monument, Jose Marti, Jose de San Martin, Seventh Regiment Memorial, William Tecumseh Sherman

SPORTS

Fred Lebow, Rowers

CHAPTER 10
Further Reading

Annual Reports of the Board of Commissioners of the Central Park on Google: https://catalog.hathitrust.org/Record/011570428 (early) and https://www.nycgovparks.org/news/reports/archive (all)

Heckscher, Morrison H. *Creating Central Park.* New York: Metropolitan Museum of Art, 2008. Focuses on the actual construction of the park. Great archival images.

Miller, Sara Cedar. *Central Park: An American Masterpiece.* New York: Harry N. Abrams and the Central Park Conservancy, 2003. A detailed history with fabulous photos.

Reed, Henry Hope, Robert M. McGee, and Esther Mipaas. *Bridges of Central Park.* New York: For the Greensward Foundation, 1990. History and sketches of each of the bridges.

CHAPTER 11
References

Note: These are also available online at

http://diannedurantewriter.com/central-park-the-early-years-references

p. 2 Amazon Author Page
   https://www.amazon.com/Dianne-L.-Durante/e/B001JS9VDO/ref=ntt_dp_epwbk_0

p. 12 (Chapter 2.3.2): Dianne L. Durante, *Dr. James Marion Sims*
   http://amzn.to/2zS0ORU

p. 18 Irish Hunger Memorial
   http://bpcparks.org/whats-here/parks/irish-hunger-memorial/

p. 21 (Fig. 23): Charles Hemstreet, *When Old New York was Young*, 1902
   https://babel.hathitrust.org/cgi/pt?id=uc1.$b630339

p. 21 (Fig. 25): Benson John Lossing, *The Hudson from the Wilderness to the Sea*, 1866
   https://www.flickr.com/photos/internetarchivebookimages/14802985963/in/photolist-dCQCRk-owiyVd-odgy12-ow1Gv6-obZr4C-oc1udt-otUjVt-otdFcg-odGZ2W-oszjNE-ouDDGh-owib41-obMFD2-ouSmZn-oy6aZV-of1Qq7-owvDPZ-ovbbT8-osBAoo-ovEii4-ouAzk7-oeQBtJ-ouhLH7-otSxLH-otho9y-owb6o3-otuvpH-oszkaS-otUrN6-odm7Bi-od9W83-oeX4AF-ouT2fa-oygug4-odgnVf-orqdYY-oe2Pvd-ov4iZ3-owD4Tz-ouhoY5-of1WXK-odA3RL-oeUCwN-ouwAky-ocTAgP-ouypU9-oy6bmX-ow8k2G-oeS3LC-oeQPY5

p. 23 (Chapter 3.1): *Fourth Annual Report of the Board of Commissioners of the Central Park, January 1861*, p. 113
   http://home2.nyc.gov/html/records/pdf/govpub/4052annual_report_manhattan_central_park_1860.pdf

p. 23 (Chapter 3.1.1): As previous, p. 117

p. 26 (Chapter 3.3): *Fourth Annual Report of the Board of Commissioners of the Central Park, January 1861*, p. 111
   http://home2.nyc.gov/html/records/pdf/govpub/4052annual_report_manhattan_central_park_1860.pdf

p. 27 (Fig. 29) Cook, *Description of the New York Central Park*
   https://archive.org/details/descriptionofnew00cooko

p. 28 (Chapter 3.3.3): *Fourth Annual Report of the Board of Commissioners of the Central Park, January 1861*, p. 112
   http://home2.nyc.gov/html/records/pdf/govpub/4052annual_report_manhattan_central_park_1860.pdf

p. 30 (Chapter 4.1): *Minutes and Annual Reports of the Board of Commissioners of Central Park*

https://www.nycgovparks.org/news/reports/archive

p. 31 (Chapter 4.1): *First Annual Report on the Improvement of the Central Park, New York*

http://home2.nyc.gov/html/records/pdf/govpub/4055annual_report_manhattan_central_park_1857.pdf

p. 32 (Chapter 4.2): farm in Staten Island

http://www.nytimes.com/2012/08/05/nyregion/a-lab-a-home-a-memory.html

p. 35 (Fig. 48) Cook, *Description of the New York Central Park*

https://archive.org/details/descriptionofnew00cooko

p. 36 (Chapter 4.4): thirty-three entries

http://home2.nyc.gov/html/records/pdf/govpub/4072architect_report_manhattan_central_park_1858.pdf

p. 37 (Fig. 50): New-York Historical Society

http://behindthescenes.nyhistory.org/wp-content/uploads/2013/06/81069_CentralPark_RinkPlan.jpg

p. 38 (Chapter 4.5): *Third Annual Report of the Board of Commissioners of the Central Park, January 1860*, p. 37

http://home2.nyc.gov/html/records/pdf/govpub/4053annual_report_manhattan_central_park_1859.pdf

p. 39 (Fig. 54): Perkins, *The Central Park,* 1864

https://archive.org/details/centralpark00guil

p. 40 (Chapter 4.5): explained in *Landscape into Cityscape; Frederick Law Olmsted's Plans for a Greater New York City.* Edited with an introductory essay and notes by Albert Fein, p. 73

https://quod.lib.umich.edu/m/moa/AGK9973.0001.001?rgn=main;view=fulltext;q1=Architecture

p. 40 (Chapter 4.5): *Fourth Annual Report of the Board of Commissioners of the Central Park, January 1861*, p. 116

http://home2.nyc.gov/html/records/pdf/govpub/4052annual_report_manhattan_central_park_1860.pdf

p. 42 (Chapter 5.1): Heckscher, *Creating Central Park,* p. 39

https://www.metmuseum.org/art/metpublications/creating_central_park

p. 42 (Chapter 5.1): *Fourth Annual Report of the Board of Commissioners of the Central Park, January 1861*, p. 114

http://home2.nyc.gov/html/records/pdf/govpub/4052annual_report_manhattan_central_park_1860.pdf

p. 47 (Chapter 5.2.3): *Fourth Annual Report of the Board of Commissioners of the Central Park, January 1861*, p. 117

http://home2.nyc.gov/html/records/pdf/govpub/4052annual_report_manhattan_central_park_1860.pdf

p. 50 (Chapter 5.3): *Fourth Annual Report of the Board of Commissioners of the Central Park, January 1861*, pp. 120-122

http://home2.nyc.gov/html/records/pdf/govpub/4052annual_report_manhattan_central_park_1860.pdf

CENTRAL PARK: THE EARLY YEARS 91

p. 57 (Fig. 83): *Twelfth Annual Report of the Board of Commissioners of the Central Park, for the Year Ending December 31, 1868*
   http://home2.nyc.gov/html/records/pdf/govpub/4086annual_report_manhattan_central_park_1868.pdf

p. 60 (Figs. 89, 90, 91): *Harper's Weekly* on the *Herald* Hoax
   http://www.museumofhoaxes.com/hoax/text/display/the_central_park_zoo_escape_text/

p. 61 Cook, *Description of the New York Central Park*
   https://archive.org/details/descriptionofnew00cooko

p. 64 (Figs. 100, 101): Winifred E. Howe, *A History of the Metropolitan Museum*, 1913
   https://archive.org/details/historyofmetropo00howe

p. 65 (Fig. 105): As previous.

p. 65 (Fig. 106) More on ForgottenDelights.com
   http://www.forgottendelights.com/MMAbuilding.html

p. 66 (Fig. 107) Hunt, *Designs for the Gateways of the Southern Entrances*
   https://archive.org/details/designsforgatewa00hunt_1

p. 68 (Chapter 6.8): *Fifth Annual Report of the Board of Commissioners of the Central Park, 1862*, pp. 125-136
   http://home2.nyc.gov/html/records/pdf/govpub/4051annual_report_manhattan_central_park_1861.pdf

p. 72 (Chapter 7.1.4): Clarence Cook, *A Description of the New York Central Park*, 1869, p. 73
   https://archive.org/details/descriptionofnew00cooko

p. 76 (Chapter 7.2): decided to set rules for sculptures; see *Third General Report of the Board of Commissioners of the Department of Public Parks for the period of Twenty Months, from May 1st, 1872, to December 31st, 1873*, pp. 13-15
   http://home2.nyc.gov/html/records/pdf/govpub/4322annual_report_nyc_dept_public_parks_1872-73_part1.pdf

p. 78 (Chapter 7.3): Halleck's "On the Death of Joseph Rodman Drake"
   http://www.bartleby.com/102/11.html

p. 78 (Chapter 7.3): Olmsted in *Minutes of the Board of Commissioners* for May 1877 to April 1878, pp. 43-48
   https://www.nycgovparks.org/pagefiles/50/Board%20of%20Commissioners%20of%20the%20NYC%20Dept%20of%20Public%20Parks%20-%20Minutes%20-%201877-1878.pdf

p. 80 (Fig. 125): Albert Bigelow Paine, *Thomas Nast: His Period and His Pictures*, 1904, p. 164
   https://archive.org/details/thomasnasthispe00paingoog

p. 81 (Fig. 127): Albert Bigelow Paine, *Thomas Nast: His Period and His Pictures*, 1904, p. 185
   https://archive.org/details/thomasnasthispe00paingoog

p. 82 (Fig. 128): as previous.

p. 83 (Chapter 8.2): Donate to the Central Park Conservancy
   https://secure.centralparknyc.org/site/SPageServer?pagename=donate&s_src=dfy18w&s_subsrc=web_slash_donate

CHAPTER 12
1865 Chromolithographs of Central Park by Louis Prang

In 1865, Louis Prang issued a set of 36 chromolithographed cards illustrating Central Park highlights, plus 12 showing New York street scenes. Each card is 4.25 x 2.5 inches. Photos of all these are courtesy William Reese Co., https://www.williamreesecompany.com/.

CENTRAL PARK: THE EARLY YEARS 93

First row: The Island, The Rustic Bridge, Entrance to Cave, The Lake.
Second row: Rustic Arbor, The Brook, Moonlight on the Lake, Cascade.
Third row: The Arch, The Ramble, Boat Landing, Marble Bridge [!] over the Lake.

First row: Rude Stairway, Abode of the Swans, The Silver Lake, Entrance to Cave from Lake.
Second row: The Tower, Ornamental Bridge, The Drive, The Bridle Path.
Third row: The Music Temple, Sunset on the Lake, Rustic Arbor, A Glimpse of the Lake

CENTRAL PARK: THE EARLY YEARS

First row: The Marble Bridge, Vine Arbor, Bust of Schiller, The Fountain
Second row: On the Ramble, near the Lake; Fancy Bridge No. 14; The Casino; Bridge at the 7th Avenue Entrance
Third row: The Cove, Rustic Bower, Rustic Arbor, Evening on the Lake

First row: Street Musician, The Drum Major, Emigrants Just Arrived, Muddy Street

Second row: The Fruit Pedlar, The Old Coin Merchant, The Street Singers, Walking Advertisement Balloon Seller

Third row: The Convoy over Broadway, On Broadway, French Nurse, Newspaper Boy, "Tribune Sir?"

www.ingramcontent.com/pod-product-compliance
Lightning Source LLC
Chambersburg PA
CBHW050603300426
44112CB00013B/2055